PROFESSOR S. KONOVALOV
Founder-Editor of *Oxford Slavonic Papers*, 1950–1967

OXFORD
SLAVONIC PAPERS

Edited by

J. L. I. FENNELL   A. E. PENNINGTON

and

I. P. FOOTE

General Editor

NEW SERIES

VOLUME XII

OXFORD UNIVERSITY PRESS

1979

6193

Oxford University Press, Walton Street, Oxford OX2 6DP

OXFORD LONDON GLASGOW
NEW YORK TORONTO MELBOURNE WELLINGTON
KUALA LUMPUR SINGAPORE HONG KONG TOKYO
DELHI BOMBAY CALCUTTA MADRAS KARACHI
NAIROBI DAR ES SALAAM CAPE TOWN

ISBN 0 19 815654 5

*Printed in Great Britain
at the University Press, Oxford
by Eric Buckley
Printer to the University*

THE editorial policy of the New Series of *Oxford Slavonic Papers* in general follows that of the original series, thirteen volumes of which appeared between the years 1950 and 1967. It is devoted to the publication of original contributions and documents relating to the languages, literatures, culture, and history of Russia and the other Slavonic countries, and appears annually towards the end of the year. Reviews of individual books are not normally included, but bibliographical and review articles are published from time to time.

The British System of Cyrillic transliteration (British Standard 2979: 1958) has been adopted, omitting diacritics and using -y to express -й, -ий, -iй, and -ый at the end of proper names, e.g. Sergey, Dostoevsky, Bely, Grozny. For philological work the International System (ISO R/9) is used.

In the present volume we pay tribute to Professor S. Konovalov, the Founder-Editor of *Oxford Slavonic Papers*, on the occasion of his eightieth birthday, by printing a full list of the contents and an index of the original series, which appeared under his editorship. We also commemorate the late Professor Robert Auty, Editor of the New Series 1968–78, with a survey of his work and the publication of his De Carle lectures.

From this volume Dr A. E. Pennington succeeds Professor Auty as Editor.

J. L. I. FENNELL
I. P. FOOTE
A. E. PENNINGTON

The Queen's College, Oxford

CONTENTS

Two Unpublished Muscovite Chronicles

By DANIEL CLARKE WAUGH

Открывателю Холмогорской летописи посвящаю

THE very numerous short Russian chronicles found largely in late
Muscovite manuscript miscellanies have understandably interested
scholars less than the larger narrative sources for the history of early
Russia.[1] Too often the short texts contain no information that is not to
be found in other sources, or if some information is unique, it is provin-
cial in focus and often trivial. None the less, even where their content
is meagre, such short texts can reveal a great deal about the process of
historical compilation (especially in the period when it is generally
accepted that chronicle writing in the strict sense was dying) and may
illuminate the activities of individual scriptoria, the study of which has
only begun. A short chronicle which illustrates these points is that
found in three seventeenth-century Muscovite miscellanies: Moscow,
State Historical Museum (GIM), Museum Collection, No. 2524
(hereafter *M*); Leningrad, Saltykov-Shchedrin Public Library (GPB),
Collection of M. P. Pogodin, No. 1573 (hereafter *P*); and Leningrad,
Library of the Academy of Sciences (BAN), 16.7.15 (hereafter *A*).[2]

The author is grateful to the Inter-University Committee on Travel and Grants and the
International Research and Exchanges Board for supporting the research which made this
article possible.

[1] For exceptions see, for example, A. A. Zimin, 'Kratkie letopistsy XV–XVI vv.', *Istori-
cheskii arkhiv*, v (1950), 3–39; Ya. S. Lur'e, 'Kratkii letopisets Pogodinskogo sobraniya',
Arkheograficheskii ezhegodnik za 1962 g. (1963), 431–44. M. N. Tikhomirov took a particular
interest in such short chronicles. See his 'Zapiski o regentstve Eleny Glinskoi i boyarskom
pravlenii 1533–1547 gg.', *Istoricheskie zapiski*, xlvi (1954), 278–88, and his valuable descriptive
catalogue, *Kratkie zametki o letopisnykh proizvedeniyakh v rukopisnykh sobraniyakh Moskvy* (M., 1962).

[2] These manuscripts are described as follows:

1. GIM, Museum Collection, No. 2524—D. C. Waugh, '*De visu* Description of Manuscripts Containing the *Correspondence*', in: E. L. Keenan, *The Kurbskii–Groznyi Apocrypha*
(Cambridge, Mass., 1971), 114–19.

2. GPB, Collection of M. P. Pogodin, No. 1573—A. F. Bychkov, *Opisanie tserkovno-
slavyanskikh i russkikh rukopisnykh sbornikov Imperatorskoi Publichnoi biblioteki*, i (Spb., 1882),
139–46 (extracts from the chronicle, pp. 139–40), and Waugh, '*De visu* Description', 126–30;
for new information concerning the composition of the miscellany of which *P* was only a part,
see D. K. Uo [D. C. Waugh], 'K izucheniyu istorii rukopisnogo sobraniya P. M. Stroeva'
(pt. 2), *Trudy Otdela drevnerusskoi literatury* (hereafter *TODRL*), xxxii (1977), 135–8.

3. BAN, 16.7.15—*Opisanie Rukopisnogo otdela Biblioteki Akademii nauk SSSR*, iii, vyp. 2
(M.-L., 1965), 210–12. G. Z. Kuntsevich prepared for publication a lengthy description of
M, which included quotation of sizeable portions of the chronicle. See the incomplete page
proofs of vol. ii of his *Sochineniya knyazya Kurbskogo*, Leningradskoe otdelenie Instituta istorii
Akademii nauk SSSR, Russkaya sektsiya, *fond* 276, *op.* 1, No. 30, pp. 224–30.

For convenience, I shall call the text the 'Chronicle of Iov Ivanov', after the owner of its earliest manuscript (*M*).

The purpose of this article is to analyse and publish the texts of the Chronicle of Iov Ivanov and of another interesting short chronicle used in its second redaction, the so-called Bezdnin Chronicle.

Compiled most probably in the middle of the seventeenth century, the Chronicle of Iov Ivanov has hitherto attracted attention primarily because it contains information about events on the Northern Dvina River in the second half of the sixteenth century and unique information (in its second redaction) about a *dumnyi dvoryanin*, M. A. Bezdnin (Beznin).[3] The chronicle has not been published in its entirety, nor have scholars observed that in two of its three manuscripts we appear to have what we might term 'author's text' (that is, for each of the two redactions). Moreover, the content and palaeographic features of these manuscripts and a number of others suggest the existence in or near Kholmogory of an important scriptorium in the middle third of the seventeenth century, one where there appears to have been a particular interest in historical compilation.

The second of the texts to be published here was named the 'Bezdnin Chronicle' by its discoverer, the late Academician M. N. Tikhomirov, because of its information on the activities of M. A. Bezdnin in 1584.[4] The portion of this chronicle copied in manuscript *M* was reworked into the text of the Chronicle of Iov Ivanov in its second redaction (in *P*).

I. THE CHRONICLE OF IOV IVANOV

The Chronicle of Iov Ivanov is found in its first redaction in manuscripts *M* and *A*, while *P* is the only copy known to me of the second redaction. As will emerge from the study which follows, *M* is the author's text, containing ample evidence of cutting and splicing from a variety of sources.[5] The seams evident in the palaeographic features of *M* have been smoothed over in *A* and *P*. The latter are, none the less, important for establishing the full text of the original, since two folios of *M* (preceding the current f. 1 and between f. 7 and f. 8) were lost between the manuscript's completion in the third quarter of the seventeenth century and its binding in the nineteenth century. There is every reason to believe that *P* and *A* reproduce accurately the missing portions of the text.

[3] Ya. S. Lur'e, 'O neizdannoi Kholmogorskoi letopisi', *Issledovaniya po otechestvennomu istochnikovedeniyu. Sbornik statei, posvyashchennykh 75-letiyu professora S. N. Valka* (M.–L., 1964), 454, n. 17; Tikhomirov, *Kratkie zametki* (n. 1), 10.

[4] Tikhomirov knew of only one full copy; I have located a second and one other fragment.

[5] Authors' texts are quite rare; see the remarks of Ya. S. Lur'e in 'Lavrent'evskaya letopis' — svod nachala XIV v.', *TODRL*, xxix (1974), 57.

At the basis of the Chronicle of Iov Ivanov is a 'core' text consisting of short entries concerning Russian—but especially Muscovite—history from the coming of Ryurik and his brothers to the late sixteenth century. While one cannot be absolutely certain which articles came from this source, it seems likely that they included the ones for the following years: 6300 (an erroneous date for the calling of Ryurik), 6496, 6666, 6745, 6875, 6888 (an erroneous date for the fall of Constantinople to the Turks), 6986, 6993, 7018, 7022, 7061, 7071, 7079(?), 7081, and 7085. Probably included as well were the entries for 7088, 7089, and the first of two entries for 7092. The entries in the text become more detailed for the later years, so that the bulk of the text is devoted to the reign of Tsar Ivan IV (1533–84) and, especially, the events of the Livonian War. If my assumption is correct about the inclusion of entries for 7088, 7089, and 7092, then the text ended at a logical point with the death of Ivan IV and the enthronement of his son, Fedor Ivanovich. I feel that the enumerated articles all come from a single source, chiefly because they follow one another in correct chronological sequence and without any palaeographic indications that they were being taken from different sources (the entry for 7079 is an exception—see below). In contrast, entries that apparently derived from different sources often were inserted in the margin by the copyist, are otherwise set off from the main text, or are found out of chronological order.

Among the entries in this core text, one is of particular interest for the unique information it contains. For 7088, the chronicle tells how a certain 'Doctor' Elisey advised Ivan IV against going to the aid of Polotsk. As a result, the Poles took the city and Ivan had the doctor executed for treasonous dealings with the enemy. As Ya. S. Lur'e has pointed out to me, the 'doctor' in question is undoubtedly the Eleazar Bomelius, whose torture and execution for treason are described in loving detail by Sir Jerome Horsey in his *Travels*.[6] We cannot be sure whether the information about Polotsk has any basis in fact, but the detail of the chronicle entry suggests that it may have been composed near the time when the 'core' text was compiled.

The entry for 7079 draws our attention because it is found in the margin of f. 3ʳ, with a note by the copyist on f. 2ʳ indicating where it should be inserted. The entry is also curious because of its content: information about a battle on the River Shelon' on 14 July 1571, in which the Novgorodians defeated the Lithuanians. I have been unable to confirm that such a battle occurred. Furthermore, I find it a rather striking coincidence that the date is so close to that of the important

[6] See L. E. Berry and R. O. Crummey (eds.), *Rude and Barbarous Kingdom: Russia in the Accounts of Sixteenth-century English Voyagers* (Madison, Milwaukee, and London, 1968), 274, 279, 292–3. Ya. S. Lur'e drew my attention to a passage in the Pskov III Chronicle, where the evil deeds of this Doctor Elisey are described somewhat differently, but with the same general thrust (*Pskovskie letopisi*, ed. A. N. Nasonov, vyp. 2 (M., 1955), 262).

victory of Grand Prince Ivan III over Novgorod on the Shelon':
14 July 1471 (6979). Could not the entry for 7079 have been made up
on the basis of confused information about the battle a century earlier?
Be that as it may, it seems likely that the copyist came across that
information only after he had begun f. 3. Either he found it in a
separate source, or, if in fact the 7079 entry was part of the core text,
he unwittingly overlooked it while inserting the entry for 7080 from a
different source and then discovered the omission when he returned to
the core text.

The entry for 7080, which concerns the Tatar invasion of 1571,
stands out because of its length—two and a half pages, in contrast to
the two-line entries that immediately precede and follow. Moreover,
unlike all the preceding articles, the entry for 7080 begins Лета,
instead of В лета. We know of a number of separate accounts in
Muscovite manuscripts concerning the Crimean invasion; while most
are longer than the one found here, clearly there is some textual connection between our entry and those accounts.[7] It seems likely that the
chronicler turned to a source other than the core text for this entry.

A second marginal insertion in manuscript M is the entry for 7087,
which gives details of a fire in Kazan'. Both the content and position
of this insertion suggest that it derives from a separate source consulted
by the copyist only after he had recorded his core text. Textually this
entry is related to one found in the later Mazurin Chronicle, two
other entries of which (see below) are also very close to ones found in
the Chronicle of Iov Ivanov.[8] Until more evidence is found, we can
only posit that the two chronicles have a common source.

Following the first entry for 7092, there are indications of irregulari-
ties in the compilation. Note the sequence of dates in the entries from
that point: 7091, 7092 (written in the margin and repeating in part the
previous entry for 7092), 7099, 7093, 7105, and 7104. Certain physical
features of the manuscript are also revealing, as the following table
summarizes:

Folios	Watermarks	Lines per page	Cinnabar	Remarks
1ʳ⁻ᵛ	Type I	17	No	A separate sheet pasted in.
2ʳ⁻4ʳ	—	18	Yes	
4ᵛ⁻5ᵛ	—	17	Yes	
6ʳ⁻ᵛ	—	8	Yes	Text ends middle of f. 6ʳ; f. 6ᵛ blank.

---

[7] The account in the chronicle could easily be a retelling of one of the texts published by
V. I. Buganov in 'Povest' o pobede nad krymskimi tatarami v 1572 godu', *Arkheograficheskii
ezhegodnik za 1961 g.* (1962), especially pp. 269–75. However, the information about the
captured Divei Mirza being taken to Novgorod is found, to the best of my knowledge, only
in the *Piskarevskii letopisets*; see *Materialy po istorii SSSR*, ii (M., 1955), 80–1. A seventeenth-
century chronicle may eventually be discovered which will prove to be the source for this
particular article in the Chronicle of Iov Ivanov.

[8] *Polnoe sobranie russkikh letopisei* (hereafter *PSRL*), xxxi (M., 1968), 142.

Folios	Watermarks	Lines per page	Cinnabar	Remarks
7^{r–v}	Type II	18	Yes	A single folio (presumably once pasted in) missing between f. 7 and f. 8.
8^{r–v}	Type II (other half of preceding)	19	Yes/No	Extra line added to bottom of f. 8^r and lacking cinnabar; f. 8^v has regular spacing and no cinnabar.
9^r–12^v	Type III	17	No	Text ends after 4 lines on f. 12^r; f. 12^v blank.

The copyist normally wrote 18 lines per page for the core text, as well as for a significant portion of the rest of the manuscript. Where he has only 17 lines per page or, more rarely, 19, there appears to have been a special reason. The easiest case to document is f. 1, which has a watermark that appears again only much later in the manuscript. With the exception of the first line (Васильевичь Казань взял), f. 1 is devoted entirely to information concerning the Northern Dvina region in the second half of the sixteenth century. The source of this information is the 'Short Chronicle of the Dvina *Voevody*', recently discovered by Ya. S. Lur'e in a manuscript containing the *Kholmogorskaya letopis'*.[9] It seems that the compiler of the Chronicle of Iov Ivanov came across this Dvina information after he had already copied the now missing first folio of his manuscript and the present ff. 2 seqq. Although he had to violate chronology in order to include the new information and not throw away what had already been copied, he was able to do so by taking only so much of the Dvina information as would fit on one page, beginning that page with the line that began the current f. 2 (in order to complete the entry for the year 7061, which began at the bottom of the now missing first folio), and then erasing that line from the top of what is now f. 2^r (the erased Васильевич Казань взял is still visible). The quotation from the 'Short Chronicle of the Dvina *Voevody*' is, incidentally, an exact copy of the beginning of that work.

We encounter once again a page (f. 4^v) with only 17 lines of text where the sequence of entries noted above (7091, 7092, etc.) begins. Unfortunately, it is here less easy to determine what material may have come from what source. Of some things, though, we can be certain. The second entry for the year 7092 undoubtedly came from a source different from that which supplied the first entry for that year. Both recount the enthronement of Fedor Ivanovich, but the dates they give differ (in the first, 28 May; in the second, 1 June; the correct date is 31 May). It is possible, but less likely, that the second of the entries came from the core account, in which case the preceding entry for

---

[9] See Ya. S. Lur'e, 'Kholmogorskaya letopis'', *TODRL*, xxv (1970), especially p. 135; K. N. Serbina, 'Dvinskii letopisets', *Vspomogatel'nye istoricheskie distsipliny*, v (1973), especially p. 207. This short chronicle of the Dvina *voevody* is published as an appendix to the *Kholmogorskaya letopis'* in *PSRL*, xxxiii (L., 1977), 145–7.

7092 would have come from a different source. Whether or not the entries that follow, for 7099 and 7093, came from the same source as that for 7092 is uncertain;[10] exactly what happened at this point in the compilation of the chronicle can probably be established only when we find more of the sources used.

The entries for 7105 and 7104 stand apart in that, like the entry for 7087, neither of them contains Moscow information. The first deals with an earthquake in Nizhny Novgorod; the second concerns the discovery of the relics of SS Gury and Varsonofy during the construction of a cathedral in Kazan'. The Nizhny Novgorod information appears to have derived originally from a Nizhny Novgorod chronicle, although in the version used by the Chronicle of Iov Ivanov it is textually almost identical with the same information reproduced in the late seventeenth-century Mazurin Chronicle.[11] Presumably, the two have a common source. The information about the discovery of the relics in Kazan' is found in a nearly contiguous passage in the Mazurin Chronicle. As with the Nizhny Novgorod entry, the texts about the Kazan' relics in the two chronicles are virtually identical—suggesting a common source, if not direct borrowing one from another. We may hypothesize that the copyist of M completed the first few pages of his chronicle, leaving the rest of one signature blank. On the blank pages (beginning with f. 4ᵛ) he then added entries from various sources, including one that contained the two items for 7105 and 7104. Following the latter he left 1½ pages blank (f. 6ʳ⁻ᵛ), because he had in hand material already copied for a continuation of the text beginning with the year 7105.

Beginning at the top of f. 7 (the paper of which is different from that of f. 6), we find that continuation—an entry on the fortification of Smolensk in 7105 and a very interesting account of the death of Fedor Ivanovich and the election of Boris Godunov in 7106. In particular, the eulogy of Fedor Ivanovich stands out for its literary quality. A very poetic text, it reminds us of a number of famous laments from early Russian literature:

Яко солнце заиде в далныя страны и земли, свеща русийская угасе, и яко камень драгий, адамант, лице свое сокры, во гроб вселися и в земли затворися, свет померче, и красный цвет християньский увяде. И яко кипарис крепкий ис корени исторжеся, и не остася отрасли ни мала от семени (f. 7ʳ⁻ᵛ).

I have not yet established its source, but I suspect that the chronicler simply adapted the lament from another work.[12]

[10] The entry for 7093 is somewhat mysterious: presumably it is referring to what other sources report under 7094, the beginning of the construction of the stone 'White City' (Белый город) 'подле земляныя осыпи' in Moscow. Cf., for example, PSRL, xxxi, 144.

[11] See A. S. Gatsisky, Nizhegorodskii letopisets (Nizhny Novgorod, 1886), 36–43; Drevnyaya rossiiskaya vivliofika, 2 ed., xviii (M., 1791), 86–7; PSRL, xxxi, 146.

[12] Cf. another rather poetic passage, under 6888, where the chronicler records: 'безбожный Махмет власть греческую погаси, яко же ветр и буря зелна вся без вести сотвори.'

At the end of the account of Boris's election, once again there is a break in the manuscript. When he began f. 8, the copyist had planned for an 18-line page. The account of the election left space for 2 lines, but we find that 3 have been written in—by the same hand, in an obviously cramped style—in order to fill the space. F. 8ᵛ likewise has an extra line, but with even spacing. From f. 9 to the end of the chronicle the pages contain only 17 lines each and the paper is different from any of the preceding folios. The text beginning at the top of f. 9ʳ (and ending on f. 12ʳ) deals with the Time of Troubles, from the death of the first false Dmitry in 1606 to the election of Mikhail Romanov in 1613, after which the chronicle jumps ahead to its last entry on Tsar Mikhail's death in 1645 (7153). Clearly, what the chronicler attempted to do on f. 8ʳ⁻ᵛ was to squeeze in whatever was necessary to provide the transition between Boris's election and the death of the false Dmitry I, either because the text beginning on f. 9 had already been copied or possibly because he simply hoped to reach a convenient stopping-point at the bottom of f. 8ᵛ (the former seems the more likely alternative).

We can identify the source for the whole passage from the enthronement of Boris to that of Mikhail Romanov. Later in *M* (ff. 173ᵛ–176ᵛ) is the text of a letter written in 1613 in the name of Tsar Mikhail Romanov to two 'Megapolinsk' princes, 'Fionmarkon' and 'Rulyak'.[13] As was common in letters during and immediately after the Time of Troubles, this one to the two French princes includes a short self-contained tale about events during the Time of Troubles. We know that many such tales were simply copied verbatim from one *gramota* to the next. Of all the accounts I have seen, the version found in the letter to Fionmarkon and Rulyak is textually closest to one included in a letter, also written in 1613, from Tsar Mikhail Fedorovich to King Louis XIII.[14] Probably the editing of the letter to King Louis to the shorter form in the letter to the princes was carried out in the Diplomatic Chancellery. The further editing of the tale for inclusion in the Chronicle of Iov Ivanov was probably done by the chronicler himself. He appears to have had access to both the letters of 1613 (that to Louis XIII is found in *P* and in GPB, F.XVII.15, manuscripts probably made in

13 On their identity, see Givi Zhordaniya, *Ocherki iz istorii franko-russkikh otnoshenii kontsa XVI i pervoi poloviny XVII vv.*, i (Tbilisi, 1959), especially pp. 339–47. The text of the letter has been published, from *P*, in *Akty istoricheskie, sobrannye i izdannye Arkheograficheskoyu kommissieyu*, iii (Spb., 1841), 4–7. The differences between copies *M* and *P* are trivial, except as noted in n. 15 below.

14 To the best of my knowledge, this letter remains unpublished. Copies are in *P* (lacking the ending) and in MS GPB, F.XVII.15, the texts of which contain only insignificant differences. A textually related but longer letter from Tsar Mikhail Fedorovich to King Louis XIII of 1615 has been published by V. N. Berkh, *Tsarstvovanie tsarya Mikhaila Fedorovicha i vzglyad na mezhdutsarstvie* (Spb., 1832), 116–59, and apparently exists in a manuscript copy in GIM, Collection of A. S. Uvarov, No. 1495 (752) (714). Textual comparison suggests that the text of 1615 was composed on the basis of the version of 1613.

the same scriptorium as *M*), yet he chose the shorter text. He probably decided to use it only when he had copied on in manuscript *M* and come across in one of his sources the letter to the French princes. At that point, he made a complete copy of the letter for the manuscript, copied also a portion of the tale about the Time of Troubles (but in contracted form), and went back to fit the parts together.[15] He then determined how much connecting text was needed (miscalculating slightly) and completed the task of editing by cramming in whatever would fit on f. 8. Significantly, the text of the full *gramota* on ff. 173^v–176^v and the extract from it inserted in the chronicle are distinct from the surrounding texts in that they contain no cinnabar initials. Moreover, the connection of the *gramota* with the editing which took place after the core text of the chronicle had been copied is suggested by the fact that the paper used for insertion of the Dvina information (see above, p. 5) reappears in the manuscript only from the section containing the text of the full *gramota*.

The nature of the editing in the account of the Time of Troubles can been seen from the following comparison of the chronicle with its source.

Chronicle of Iov Ivanov	*Letter to Fionmarkon and Rulyak*
И при его державе, по вражью действу, а по злому умышленью, и по ненависти полского и литовского Жигимонта короля и панов рад, через многое его королевское крестное целованье, в Московъском государстве смута и межусобье учинилася. Некоторой вор, чернец, еретик, имянем Гришка Отрепьев, за некоторые богомерские его дела, с Москвы збежал в Литву, и свергл с себя черное платье, назвался царевичем Дмитреем углецким, великого государя, царя Ивана Васильевича всеа Русии сыном . . . (f. 8^{r-v}).	И при его державе, по вражью действу, а по злому умышленью, и по ненависти полского и литовского Жигимонта короля и панов рад, через многое его королевское *и панов рад* крестное целованье, в *нашем* Московском государстве смута и межусобье учинилося. Некоторой вор, чернец, еретик, имянем Гришка Отрепьев, за некоторые богомерские *и скаредные свои* дела, *из Московского государства* збежал в Литву, и свергл с себя черное платье, *и аггельский образ обруга, и врагом рукописание на себя дав, аще коснется царьского, то от Бога отлучен будет,* назвался царевичем Дмитреем углетцким, великого государя *блаженныя памяти* царя *и великого князя* Ивана Васильевича всеа Русии *самодержца* сыном . . . (f. 174^v).

[15] While the letter is found in *P* in a copy nearly identical with that of *M*, one should note that a few readings suggest that the chronicler used the copy in *M* or its immediate protograph as his source rather than the copy in *P*.

For the most part, the chronicler simply omitted titles, extra epithets, parts of lists, and the like. There seems to have been no effort to change the sense of the text. When he reached the point where the letter referred to the Tsar in the first person, the chronicler changed that to the third person; he also added the date of the election of the first Romanov, something that was not needed at the same point in the letter, which was properly dated at the end. One could, of course, question whether the indicated changes are decisive in proving the direction of borrowing that I have indicated. Assuming the authenticity of the letter and given the other facts available concerning manuscript *M* and the author's text of the chronicle, a reverse relationship seems very unlikely.

The first redaction of the Chronicle of Iov Ivanov seems to have existed in at least one seventeenth-century copy that has not come down to us. The evidence for this is provided by the late seventeenth-century copy *A*, which derived from a copy which lacked one folio. The copyist of *A* simply wrote on, regardless of the break.[16] Otherwise *A* reproduces the full text of the first redaction, including the portion at the beginning and a later one which are now lost in *M* because of missing folios. *A* or its original did improve *M* in one respect, by placing the entries for 7093 and 7099 in correct chronological order. Also, the marginal notations of *M* were inserted in their proper places and the text copied through without leaving empty spaces. Manuscript *A* is, though, somewhat carelessly copied; furthermore, it is occasionally difficult to determine its original readings, since someone in the eighteenth century undertook to correct some of the mistakes in copying as well as some errors in dating that appear to have been present in the original chronicle.[17] In using *A* for variant readings, I have therefore attempted to give only those readings that were in the original seventeenth-century text of that copy.

Unlike *A*, manuscript *P* is probably contemporary with *M*. Moreover, there is evidence that the copyists of *P* may have had direct access to *M*, since the editing that they undertook to form the second redaction of the Chronicle of Iov Ivanov reflects knowledge of another text contained in *M*.[18] In particular, we note in *P* two insertions, one for 7079 and the other for 7092. The first of these, concerning the burning of Moscow in 1571 by the Tatars, is inserted in correct chronological

---

[16] The passage in question in *A* is: 'Лета 7089 литовской король Стефан Оботур приходил к государеву, цареву и великого князя городу. Лета 7091-го свейской король Ругодив взяли[!]' (BAN, 16.7.15, f. 85ʳ).

[17] This hand of the marginal notations (and apparently the corrections) in the chronicle is identified in *Opisanie Rukopisnogo otdela BAN SSSR*, iii, vyp. 2, pp. 210, 212, as that of an army corporal, S. K. Smirnov.

[18] I specify copyists, because the hand changes on f. 14ʳ beginning with the entry for 7089. It appears that the second hand is the one which added the headings throughout the manuscript.

sequence. The second, concerning the activities of Mikhail Andreevich Bezdnin, is inserted out of sequence, between the entries for 7105 and 7106. In *M* both texts are found not in the Chronicle of Iov Ivanov (ff. 1–12), but in another short chronicle copied in the same manuscript on ff. 73ᵛ–76ʳ. That text is a portion of the Bezdnin Chronicle, the features of which I shall discuss below. In using the Bezdnin Chronicle, the copyists of *P* extracted information they did not already have in their basic text. The only change made in the borrowed material was the replacement of В лета 7079-го with Того же году (there was already an entry for 7079), and Того же лета with В лета 7092-го (there being no indication of the date in the preceding text). That this editing was done by the copyists of *P* is supported by the fact that three additional items of information from the text of ff. 73ᵛ–76ʳ in *M* were inserted in *P* by its second scribe after he had already completed the copying of his text.[19]

Another feature of *P* which distinguishes the second redaction is the omission of the tale about the Time of Troubles. *P* concludes with two short entries on the death of Fedor Ivanovich and the accession of Boris Godunov. It seems likely that the two were created simply by contracting a longer entry in the first redaction of the Chronicle of Iov Ivanov:

First Redaction (*M*)	Second Redaction (*P*)
Лета 7106-го генваря в 7 день преставися царь и великий князь Федор Ивановичь московский и всеа Русии, удобрение и само-держец государства Московъ-ского, своея великия отчины, и многих государств обладатель, в 13 лето государства его. Яко солнце заиде . . . . В лета 7107 сентября в 3 день по велению царицы . . . и по благословению . . . Иова патриарха московъского . . . поставлен бысть на Москве Богом избранный государь, царь и вели-кий князь Борис Федоровичь на превелицем престоле царства Московъскаго . . . (ff. 7ʳ–8ʳ).	В лето 7106-го генваря в 7 день преставися царь и великий князь Федор Ивановичь московский и всеа Русии, в 13 лето государства своего. [В л]ета 7107-го сентября в 3 день восприят скипетр [Москов]-ского государства и многих государств всеа [Русии] Борис Федоровичь Годунов (f. 16ʳ–ᵛ).

The reason for the contraction of the first redaction by *P* is easy to find. Later in *P* the copyist(s) included not only the letter of Tsar Mikhail Fedorovich to Fionmarkon and Rulyak, but also the Tsar's

---

[19] See the reproduction of f. 14ᵛ in Waugh, '*De visu* Description' (n. 2), 127, and the discussion there.

letter to King Louis XIII. Both texts contain accounts of the Time of Troubles, which, as we already know, were more detailed than that in the Chronicle of Iov Ivanov. Moreover, *P* as it now stands is only part of a much larger manuscript, which contained, *inter alia*, two long and well-known accounts of the Time of Troubles, the so-called *Inoe skazanie* and the account written by the monk Avraamy Palitsyn.[20] To add yet another account which merely duplicated material to be included later in the manuscript clearly seemed to the editor pointless.

The final change made in the Chronicle of Iov Ivanov by the author(s) of its second redaction was to remove the account of the Nizhny Novgorod earthquake and to make of it a longer and separate tale, which was then placed at the end of the chronicle. In expanding the description of the earthquake, the author of this new text seems to have taken as his main source an account very close to that found in a late seventeenth-century Nizhny Novgorod chronicle.[21] He began by using the Chronicle of Iov Ivanov (Печерский трус бысть . . .), switched to the new source briefly (от монастыря к конюшенному двору . . .), returned to the Chronicle of Iov Ivanov (преж сего по летописцем . . .), and then filled in with details from his second source (Тако же ныне в наша лета . . .). Finally, the author of the text in *P* added references to an earthquake in Constantinople in the time of Emperor Justinian and another in Antioch as further evidence of the power of God's wrath. The source for these items was probably a Chronograph.[22]

I have attempted to summarize in the accompanying stemma the relationships among copies *M*, *A*, and *P* of the Chronicle of Iov Ivanov and their sources. That portion of the stemma dealing with the Dvina chronicle information may well become more complex than depicted; similarly, an investigation of the sources for the Mazurin Chronicle would undoubtedly provide a somewhat more complex scheme for the transmission of the entries on Kazan' and Nizhny Novgorod (for 7104 and 7105). The hypothesized copy of the letter to the Megapolinsk princes which served as a source for *M* and *P* is probably part of a large manuscript miscellany that contained also other works found in both *M* and *P*. However, since they are not directly related to the problem under discussion, I have not attempted to include these items in the diagram.

[20] Details are in my 'K izucheniyu' (n. 2); the two long works about the Time of Troubles are now in MS GPB, Collection of M. P. Pogodin, No. 1503.

[21] See the texts published in Gatsisky, op. cit. (n. 11), especially pp. 36–9, and in *Drevnyaya rossiiskaya vivliofika*, loc. cit. (n. 11). One should note that the seventeenth-century Russian chronicles record under 7104 a different version of the account of what appears to be the same earthquake. Textually, this second account is related to that of the Nizhny Novgorod Chronicle for 7105. Cf. *PSRL*, xiv (*Novyi letopisets*), 48–9, and xxxi (Mazurin Chronicle), 146.

[22] Both earthquakes are recorded in the 'Chronograph of 1512', which in turn took the information from a Byzantine chronicle. See *PSRL*, xxii (1), 295. The text of the Chronograph in that version lacks details included in the account of *P*.

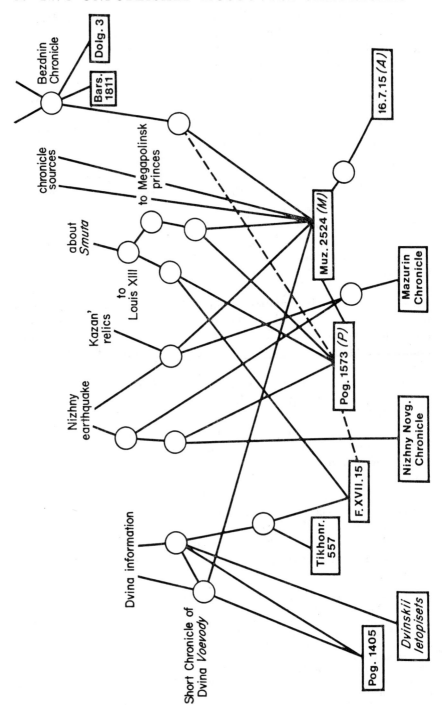

A few words should be said about the date and provenance of the Chronicle of Iov Ivanov. The death of Tsar Mikhail Fedorovich in 1645 is a *terminus a quo* for the compilation; the paper of *M* suggests that it was copied in the mid 1650s or somewhat later. Several facts point to the work having been done in a scriptorium in Kholmogory. The two owners recorded in the inscriptions on *M* were Kholmogory priests associated with the most important churches of the town. The inclusion of information from the Dvina chronicle also suggests provenance from that region of Muscovy. Moreover, related Dvina chronicle extracts are found in several other manuscripts, as indicated in the stemma.[23] Some of those manuscripts have clear associations with the Dvina region, as revealed by owners' inscriptions; all have palaeographic features connecting them with *M* and *P*. Inscriptions and similarities in handwriting suggest that certain other seventeenth-century manuscripts may also be linked with this group.[24] While further study of all these related manuscripts is needed, and others undoubtedly will be found, the evidence I have seen so far indicates that they may be the products of an important but hitherto ignored scriptorium in the Russian north, one which contained an extensive library of Muscovite secular literature. Possibly, that scriptorium was associated with the main (Preobra-zhenskii) cathedral in Kholmogory in the period between 1650 and 1680.

II. THE BEZDNIN CHRONICLE

The Bezdnin Chronicle is contained in full in two manuscripts: GBL, *fond* 92, Collection of S. O. Dolgov, No. 3 (Museum Collection, No. 5890); GIM, Collection of E. V. Barsov, No. 1811.[25] Both manuscripts

[23] The manuscripts are: GPB, Collection of M. P. Pogodin, No. 1405, the bulk of which is taken up by the *Kholmogorskaya letopis'*, to which is appended the short chronicle of the Dvina *voevody*; GPB, F.XVII.15, a miscellany containing an interesting collection of secular literature, including several works found in *P*; State Lenin Library of the USSR (GBL), Collection of N. S. Tikhonravov, No. 557, a historical compilation which uses in part the *Stepennaya kniga*.

[24] Among them are: GIM, Collection of the Synodal (Patriarchal) Library, No. 127/77, the copy of the 'Cosmography of 1670' made in Kholmogory (see the facsimile of the hand on the cover of *Kozmografiya 1670 g.* (Izdaniya Obshchestva lyubitelei drevnei pis'mennosti, xxi, lvii, lxviii (Spb., 1878–81)); BAN, 32.8.4, containing a 'Book of Degrees' (*Stepennaya kniga*)— see pl. [11] and [12] in G. N. Moiseeva, *Lomonosov i drevnerusskaya literatura* (L., 1971). MS GIM, Collection of Count A. S. Uvarov, No. 1844 (756) may also be associated with this group: this possibility should be checked, since I was unable to include it in my palaeographic comparison based on samples of the hands in other manuscripts. Unfortunately, limitations of space do not permit me to include the details of that study here.

[25] A brief description of the two manuscripts is as follows:
1. GBL, Collection of S. O. Dolgov, No. 3, late sixteenth or early seventeenth century, 4°, 12 ff., unbound. The date may best be approximated on the basis of the paper and handwriting. The hand is a single cursive; the paper includes at least two small pot watermarks, one with a single handle and rosette top with the letter G(?) on the side, and the second an apparently single-handled pot, with the letters PB/O on the side. It is possible that the latter is a variant of the one depicted in E. Heawood, *Watermarks Mainly of the Seventeenth and Eighteenth Centuries* (Monumenta Chartae Papyraceae Historiam Illustrantia, 1) (Hilversum,

are similar in appearance and date (late sixteenth or early seventeenth century); it may be that they have a common provenance. A portion of the chronicle is also found in GIM, Museum Collection, No. 2524, ff. 73^v–76^r.

In content, the Bezdnin Chronicle resembles any number of other short chronicles compiled in Muscovy, especially those which have been found in miscellanies from monastery libraries. There is a heavy emphasis on events involving the Orthodox Church: the appointment and death of metropolitans, the death of important abbots, and so on. However, there is no concentration on a single monastery: the Troitse-Sergiev, St. Kirillo-Belozerskii, Chudov, and other monasteries are all mentioned. It does seem likely, however, that we should associate the compilation with a monastery close to Moscow. In particular, one notes that the final entry concerns the fact that the visiting Patriarch of Antioch dined in the Chudov Monastery in 1586. The chronicle is full of events concerning the dynasty of the Moscow princes—births, deaths, marriages, conquests, etc., most of them recorded very laconically.

In the portion of the chronicle dealing with the period before the mid-sixteenth century, two articles stand out because of their length. The first, for the year 6496, recounts the establishment of the church hierarchy in the time of St. Vladimir. The text of this entry is very close to that found in a short chronicle compiled in the Kirillo-Belozerskii Monastery apparently by the elder Efrosin at the end of the fifteenth century.[26] In fact, a number of other entries in the Bezdnin Chronicle are also found (usually with somewhat different wording or detail) in

1950), No. 3575 (1608). However, since this is found only on f. 12, one should be cautious in using it to date the portion of the manuscript that contains the chronicle text. The chronicle occupies ff. 1^r–11^v, with a space left at the bottom of f. 11^v. On f. 12^v, which is otherwise blank, is a partially legible eighteenth-century inscription, dated 31 Aug. 1711, apparently containing some kind of tongue-twister. The first folio of the manuscript is damaged and quite dirty, suggesting that the manuscript lay around unbound and, if connected with a larger manuscript, came at the beginning of it.

2. GIM, Collection of E. V. Barsov, No. 1811, late sixteenth or early seventeenth century, 4^0, 12 ff., unbound. As with the Dolgov copy, dating is only approximate. The hand is a Muscovite cursive, very similar to that of the Dolgov copy. The paper includes two variants of a small single-handled pot, topped by a crown with a rosette and with letters IA on the side. Pencilled on the paper wrapper of the manuscript is a note, dated 1941, by M. Shch. (presumably Marfa Vyacheslavna Shchepkina): 'к. XVI в. по почерку и вод. зн.'. The chronicle occupies ff. 1^r–12^v, with one line left blank on f. 12^v. The manuscript may at one time have been the beginning of a larger one, as there are contemporary signatures, f. 1 = 1, and f. 9 = 2. Note that in the brief description by Tikhomirov, *Kratkie zametki* (n. 1), 10, references to watermarks in Briquet's *Les Filigranes* are useful only for approximating the type of those found in the manuscript and not for precise identification.

[26] What turns out to be the second half of that chronicle and the one of the greatest interest to use, because it contains the material pertaining to Russian history, is published in Zimin, 'Kratkie letopistsy' (n. 1), 22–7 (see especially pp. 26–7). Regarding the other half of the chronicle, see R. P. Dmitrieva, 'Vzaimootnoshenie spiskov "Zadonshchiny" i tekst "Slova o polku Igoreve"' in: *Slovo o polku Igoreve i pamyatniki Kulikovskogo tsikla* (M.–L., 1966), 251, n. 78.

Efrosin's chronicle.[27] Given the fact that such material could have been compiled independently from a number of sources, it would be precipitate to suggest a direct textual link between Efrosin's compilation and the Bezdnin one until further work has been done on the many short chronicles of Muscovy. The second article that stands out for its length is that for 6938 concerning the gathering in Lithuania summoned by Grand Prince Vitovt, at which were present not only the Lithuanian and Polish magnates and church leaders but also a host of foreign dignitaries, among them the Metropolitan and the Grand Prince of Moscow. A number of chronicles record this event, but none that I have found includes all the details of the Bezdnin Chronicle (especially concerning the presence of a Wallachian *voevoda*, Stefan, and the archbishops of Cracow, Vil'na and Polotsk, and regarding Vitovt's order that those present have their living expenses provided until they left the country).[28] It is not clear why such a lengthy entry, consisting largely of a list of dignitaries who attended, was included among the short entries of this portion of the chronicle, nor can one say for sure what its source was.

The Bezdnin Chronicle is of particular interest to us for the material it contains near its end under the year 7092. It is here that we encounter Mikhail Andreevich Bezdnin (or Beznin) fighting successfully against the Tatars, and then boldly confronting an unruly crowd in front of the Kremlin and persuading it to disperse. Bezdnin, a *dvoryanin* whom we first encounter in documentary sources in 1550, had a successful and active service career until around 1589.[29] His military service saw him fighting in the west during the Livonian War and on the southern and eastern borders against the Tatars. In the 1580s he was engaged in the reception of foreign ambassadors; it is during this same period that we find him involved in a number of *mestnichestvo* disputes, most of which seem to have been settled in his favour. The *razryadnye knigi*, in which one finds an extensive record of Bezdnin's service, contain no direct evidence of the events recorded in our short chronicle for the year 7092. The only other reference I have found to the campaign against the Tatars and Bezdnin's leading role in it is in an obviously fictionalized and uncertainly dated account in the *Novyi letopisets*, a work compiled

[27] See, for example, his entries for 6745, 6816, 6862, 6888, 6890, 6900, 6918, 6935, 6936, 6939, 6917, 6942, and, at the end also out of chronological order, 6953; in Zimin, 'Kratkie letopistsy' (n. 1), 22–7.

[28] What should be the earliest version of this entry is in the Nikanor and Vologda–Perm' Chronicles (*PSRL*, xxvi, 186, and xxvii, 102). A second version—one that is closer to the Bezdnin Chronicle text—is in the Contracted *Svod* of 1493 and the texts dependent on it (*PSRL*, xxvii, 269).

[29] On his career, see V. B. Nirbok, 'Mikhail Beznin — oprichnik, monakh, avantyurist', *Voprosy istorii*, 1965, No. 11, pp. 214–16; S. P. Mordovina and A. L. Stanislavsky, 'Sostav osobogo dvora Ivana IV v period "velikogo knyazheniya" Simeona Bekbulatovicha', *Arkheograficheskii ezhegodnik za 1976 g.* (1977), 181. His last recorded function was to receive a Crimean tsarevich in February 7097 (1589)—see *Razryadnaya kniga 1559–1605 gg.*, ed. L. F. Kuz'mina and V. I. Buganov (M., 1974), 245.

in the 1620s.[30] There Bezdnin is the only military commander mentioned; his victory comes in response to a prophetic command of Tsar Fedor Ivanovich: 'Go, slaughter all the Tatars'. This account and that in the Bezdnin Chronicle could well have a common source; the *Novyi letopisets* could even have used the Bezdnin text. However, we have insufficient material to prove such a relationship.

The Moscow rebellion of 1584 is recorded in the *Novyi letopisets* and the early seventeenth-century *Piskarevskii letopisets* at greater length than we find in the Bezdnin compilation.[31] The mention of Bezdnin in connection with the rebellion is unique to the Bezdnin Chronicle: whereas there we find him and the *dumnyi d'yak* Andrey Shchelkalov pacifying the mob, in the Piskarev Chronicle we learn only that the boyars somehow settled their differences and that certain of them— unnamed—went to the Frolov Gate to quieten the crowd. The *Novyi letopisets* names Shchelkalov and others, and creates quite a dramatic scene of the crowd's shouting for the head of Bogdan Bel'sky. However, Bezdnin is absent in that version too.

As Academician Tikhomirov suggested, we might logically conclude that the Bezdnin Chronicle is somehow to be associated with the Bezdnin family.[32] We might go one step further and hypothesize that Mikhail Andreevich Bezdnin himself had something to do with the chronicle's compilation. So far I have been unable to determine the circumstances which brought Bezdnin's service career to an end (one may guess that he fell victim to one of the purges carried out by Godunov). In any event, after 1589 he is no longer recorded as being in state service. In 1591, though, there appears in our sources an elder of the Volokolamsk Monastery, Misail Beznin, who has been identified as the same individual.[33] It is of some interest that this newly appeared elder seems to have occupied a prominent place in that monastery's affairs. But at some time in the mid 1590s he appears to have quarrelled with his fellow monks.[34] The next (and so far, the last) place where I have encountered the elder Misail Beznin is as one of the signatories, this time for the Troitse-Sergiev Monastery, of the charter confirming the election of Boris Godunov in 1598.[35] The *dumnyi dvoryanin* Bezdnin thus appears to have spent his last years in a monastery. And it is in monasteries that short chronicles most closely resembling in content the

---

[30] *PSRL*, xiv, 48.

[31] Ibid. 35; *Materialy po istorii SSSR*, ii (n. 7), 87.

[32] Tikhomirov, *Kratkie zametki* (n. 1), 10.

[33] See *Akty feodal'nogo zemlevladeniya i khozyaistva* (hereafter *AFZKh*), ii, ed. A. A. Zimin (M., 1956), 437, 440, 446, 456, 492. Cf. Nirbok's assertion, without precise documentation, that Bezdnin is recorded in the documents of Volokolamsk Monastery as early as August 1586 ('Mikhail Beznin' (n. 29), 215).

[34] *AFZKh*, ii (n. 33), 456.

[35] *Akty, sobrannye v bibliotekakh i arkhivakh Rossiiskoi imperii Arkheograficheskoyu ekspeditsieyu Imperatorskoi Akademii nauk*, ii (Spb., 1836), 42, 47.

Bezdnin Chronicle were compiled. True, as I have already suggested, there is no one monastery that is singled out for particular attention in the Bezdnin Chronicle, but other short monastery chronicles do not always focus merely on local news. I would suggest then that the Bezdnin Chronicle, which ends with an item for 1586 and is found in manuscripts which might be dated as early as the 1590s, may have been compiled in one of the monasteries housing the *starets* Misail and possibly by the elder himself. If such is the case, then a search for texts that may be related directly to this compilation might begin in the collections from the Volokolamsk and Troitse-Sergiev Monasteries.

Alternatively, one might argue that the chronicle was undoubtedly completed in the 1580s, before Bezdnin's disgrace. If such were the case, one would have an explanation of why his role in the events of 1584 was singled out (whereas the silence of later sources could reflect censorship connected with knowledge of his subsequent career). Another argument in favour of the compilation dating from the 1580s is that any chronicler so intensely interested in church affairs would hardly have remained silent about the establishment of the Patriarchate in 1589, if writing after that event. The final item in the chronicle concerning the visit of the Patriarch of Antioch to the Chudov Monastery in 1586 has a kind of immediacy to it that might point us toward that monastery as the place of compilation, even though otherwise the Chudov Monastery is by no means singled out by the chronicler. Clearly, on the matter of provenance as well as on the question of how the chronicle found its way to Kholmogory in the middle of the seventeenth century, we are still unable to provide definite answers.

In preparing the critical text of the Bezdnin Chronicle, I have used as my base copy GBL, Dolgov, No. 3. There is really little to choose, though, between that copy and the one in GIM, Barsov, No. 1811. The number of copyist's errors and minor additions or omissions in each is about the same. The Dolgov copy does include one entry (for 7024) not found in the Barsov copy. I have no way of ascertaining whether that entry was part of the protograph for the two manuscripts, but in the absence of information to the contrary I have included it as part of the text. The fragment of the chronicle found in GIM, Museum Collection, No. 2524 is removed by a considerable time, and presumably by intermediary copies, from the two full copies and the protograph; it is clearly inferior to the copies in the earlier manuscripts.

TEXTS

The texts have been prepared according to the form used in *TODRL*, with the standard substitutions for Slavonic letters but preserving the original orthography and noting all but purely orthographic variants from the second and third copies. Notes designated by letters pertain to peculiarities of the published copy; notes with numerical superscripts pertain to the other copies.

THE CHRONICLE OF IOV IVANOV

Text given according to MS GIM, Museum Collection, No. 2524 (abbreviated *M*), with variants from MSS GPB, Collection of M. P. Pogodin, No. 1573 (abbreviated *P*) and BAN, 16.7.15 (abbreviated *A*).

[л. 11]ª, 36 В лета 6300³⁷ избрашася три брата от немец: Рюрик, Синеус, Трувор.³⁸ Рюрик убо седе в Новегороде, а Синеус на Белеозере, а Трувор во Изборске.

В лета 6496-го крестися Владимер киевский.

В лета 6666-го³⁹ постави град Москву князь Юрьйᵇ Владимирович.

В лета 6745-го приходил царь Батый, и грех ради наших всю землю поплени.

В лета 6875-го князь великий Дмитрей Ивановичь Донский основа Москву град каменной на успех при митрополите Алексеи апреля в 5 день.

В лета 6888-го⁴⁰ месяца⁴¹ маия при царе Констянтине нарицаемаго Дрогоса, грех ради наших, народа християнского, безбожный Махмет власть греческую погаси, яко же ветр и⁴² буря зелна вся без вести сотвори. А всех царей || [л. 11 об.] [г]реческихᶜ от великого царя Констянтина до турского взятия 86.⁴³ Последний царь Констянтин сын Мануилов,⁴⁴ сего убиша турки.

Лета 6986-го князь великий Иван Васильевичь⁴⁵ Новъград великий за себя взял.ᵈ, ⁴⁶

В лета 6993-го князь великий Иван Тверь взял.

В лета 7018-го князь великий Иван Васильевичь Псков взял генваря в 24 день.

В лета 7022 князь великий Василей Смоленск взял.

В лета 7061-го царь и великий князь Иванª || [л. 1] Васильевичьᵉ Казань взял.

В том же году был на Двине наместник князь Семен Микулинской а Пунков. Той жеᶠ и оброк збирал на себя, а дань государю збирал. А как он к⁴⁷ Москве сьехал, и после были выборной голова колмогорской а с ним Двинсково уезду судьи, ⁴⁸и судили⁴⁸ на Колмогорах верхние ⁴⁹и нижные⁴⁹ половины.⁵⁰

ᵃ⁻ᵃ Text from *P*; omitted in *M*.   ᵇ Corrected from *A*; in *P* Юрье.   ᶜ Corner of page torn off.   ᵈ Written in the margin in a different hand.   ᵉ *M* begins here.   ᶠ Corrected from *A*; in *M* and *P* тоже.

---

³⁶ *A* adds О начале русской земли.   ³⁷ 6370 *A*.   ³⁸ Трувов *A*; corrected later to Трувор.   ³⁹ 6664-го *A* (apparently a later correction).   ⁴⁰ 6960-го *A* (apparently a later correction).   ⁴¹ Omitted *A*.   ⁴² или *A*.   ⁴³ *A* adds было, а.   ⁴⁴ *A* adds было.   ⁴⁵ *A* adds взял.   ⁴⁶ Omitted *A*.   ⁴⁷ с *P*.   ⁴⁸ осудили *A*.   ⁴⁹ онижные *A*.   ⁵⁰ половинь *A*.

И[51] в 62-м году пришел аглинской карабль проведывать[52] двинсково устья и зашол в Унскую губу и зимовал. И судьи о том писали ко государю, а немец поили и кормили на Колмогорах, а отпуску им не было.

И[53] в 63-м году пришли[54] на двинское устье аглинских четыре карабли.‖ [л. 1 об.] А вологоцкие суды с немецкими товары ходили х караблям на корельское устье и по 95-й год.

А в 92-м году присланы с Москвы[55] на Двину воеводы Петр Афонасьевичь Нащекин да Залешанин Никифорович Волохов, и Архангельской город поставили однем годом и сьехали к Москве. И после того присланы на Двину приказные дети боярьские.

В 93-м году пришли к Архангельскому городу галанские карабли, а на них торговые иноземцы Ондреянов брат Тимоха с товарыщи.

А в 95-м году пришли к городу аглинские карабли. ‖ [л. 2]

[g]В лета 7071 царь Иван Васильевичь Полотеск взял.[h]

[i]В лета 7079-го июля в 14 день на Шелоне бой был. Новгородцы литовских людей побили и воевод взяли.[i, 56]

Лета 7080-го крымской царь Девлет Кирей пришел на государеву, цареву и великого князя землю московъскую с великим собранием, а хотел Москву засесть. И пришел к реке Оке, и государя, царя и великого князя Ивана Васильевича всеа Русии слуга и воевода князь Михаило Ивановичь Воротынской и иные государевы воеводы со многими людьми царя встретили у реки Оки под Серпуховым на перевозе[57] и дело с ним делали, и многих татар побили, а иных[58] множество потонуло и во многих местех. И пошел царь к Москве со всеми людьми а в розгон людей не ‖ [л. 2 об.] роспустил. И воеводы князь Михаило Воротынской с товарыщи пошли за царем к Москве и взяли с собою город гуляй, что обоз именуетца, и с[59] снарядом[60] и с пушками. И сошли царя у Воскресения в Молодех, и обоз поставили. И сведал царь, что за ним московские воеводы пришли, и воротился[61] со всеми своими людьми на московских воевод. И пришли ко обозу с великою яростию, и[62] учали приступати накрепко. И Божиим милосердием и пречистые Богородицы и святых руских чюдотворцов молитвами, воеводы на том деле убили у царя да у сынов его царевичев и ширинъских князей шурью его и мурз и татар многих, и[63] большего ‖ [л. 3] воеводу Дивия мурзу [64]Нагайсково да Казанъския[64] орды царевича в[j] живых взяли. И стоял царь у обозу у воевод 6 дней и, не ходя к Москве, воротился в Крым[65] со всем своим[66]

---

[g] One line erased: Васильевичь Казань взял.   [h] Added in the same hand in cinnabar a mark and the note приступ на поле, after which is written in a different hand на друг[ом] лист[е].   [i–i] Written at the bottom of f. 3[r] in the margin by the same hand, following a mark like that added on f. 2[r].   [j] Corrected from A; omitted in M and P.

---

[51] А Р.   [52] проповедывать А.   [53] А Р.   [54] А adds и.   [55] Москве Р.

[56] The second redaction (P) adds Того же году в приход крымскаго царя Девлет Кирея Москва вся погорела, а Москвы не взял, побежал Божиим гневом гоним. В той же пожар преставися князь Иван Дмитреевич Белской з дыму и от великаго пожару, а был ранен во многих местех от татар, месяца мая в 24 день; P then adds В.   [57] порозе Р.   [58] ных А; corrected later to иных.   [59] Omitted А.

[60] санарядом А.   [61] воротилися А.   [62] Omitted А.   [63] а А.

[64–64] Нагайской во Дазанския (later corrected to Казанския) А.   [65] Рым (later corrected to Крым) А.   [66] свом (later corrected to своим) А.

войском посрамлен, а полону рускаго не взяли никого. А Диви мурзу послали воеводы ко государю, царю и великому князю Ивану Васильевичю всеа Русии в великий Новъгород. А казацкие орды царевичь был больно ранен; держали его до государя на Москве.

В лета 7081-го царь Иван Васильевичь Пайду взял.

В лета 7085-го царь Иван Васильевичь Кесь с товарыщи взял.

[k]В лета 7087-го июня[67] в 23 день в полуденное время в Казани пожар бысть[68] велик. Загореся[69] у Николы Тульскаго, и ряды все и гостин двор и в каменном городе митрополичь двор все[70] выгорело,[71] мала[72] часть посаду остася.[k]

В лета 7088-го литовъской король ‖ [л. 3 об.] Стефан Оботур приходил к Полтъску и Полтеск взял, и владыку Киприяна и воевод поимал и людей побил. А царь и великий князь Иван Васильевичь всеа Русии в то время был во Пскове, и не велел ему против короля ити немчин, доктор Елисей, норовил литовъскому королю, и государь, царь, и великий князь Иван Васильевич [l]всеа Русии[l], [73] за то его казнил смертью.

Того же лета литовские люди взяли городок[74] Сокол, а людей московских побили.

Лета 7089-го литовской король Стефан Оботур приходил к государеву, цареву и великого князя городу ко Пскову[75] ‖ [л. 4] [76]и стоял под городом полгоду, и был в то время во Пскове наместник и воевода, князь Иван Петрович Шуйской. Город отстоял и литовских людей вылазя, побивали много. И ходил от государя, царя и великаго князя Ивана Васильевича всеа Русии к литовскому королю к Оботуру посол князь Дмитрей Елецкой. Сменял городы: московской государь взял Луки Великие, а литовской король взял немецкие городы.

Того же лета ноября в 18 день преставися царевич князь Иван Иванович в слободе Александровъской, и привезен на Москву и положен в церкви арханггела Михаила в приделе.[77]

Лета 7092-го марта в 18 день преставися царь и великий князь Иван Васильевич ‖ [л. 4 об.] московский[78] всеа Русии, во иноцех Иона, и положен на Москве в церкви архаггела же Михаила в том же приделе.[79]

Того же лета маия в 28 день[80] поставлен бысть на превелицем престоле царства Московъскаго, и Владимирском и Казанском и Астороханском и многих государств великия Русии царевич князь Федор Иванович, и венчан венцем царским, и помазан святым миром.[76]

Лета 7091-го свейской король Ругодив взял.[81]

[m]В лета 7092-го государь, царь и великий князь Федор Иванович всеа Русии седе на царство Московъское и венчася царским венцем июня в[82] 1 день.[m]

[k–k] Added in the margin in the same hand.   [l–l] Repeated, the second time having been crossed out.   [m–m] Written in the margin by the same hand.

[67] июля A.   [68] был P.   [69] загорелося A; загорел P.   [70] Omitted A.
[71] A adds же и.   [72] малая A.   [73] A adds и.   [74] город P.   [75] Added later in margin in A.   [76–76] Omitted A.   [77] Added in second redaction (P): жил 29 лет, 7 месяц.   [78] P adds и.   [79] Added in second redaction (P): жил 53 лета, 7 месяц.   [80] P adds in margin в 31 день.   [81] взяли A; added in margin in different hand B лето 7091-е государевым повелением донской атаман Ермак Тимофеев взял Сибирское царство P.   [82] Omitted A.

[83]В лета 7099-го приходил к Москве крымский царь, и Божиим милосердием государевы воеводы царя побили.[83] ‖ [л. 5]

В лета 7093-го во царство Феодора Ивановича всеа Русии основан бысть на Москве град каменной[84] около землянова града маиа в 9 день.

[85]В лета 7105-го при благочестивом царе Феодоре Ивановиче июня в 18 день в 3-м часу ночи, в Нижнем Новеграде в Печерском монастыре бысть потрясение монастырю. Многия келии повалялися, и храм[86] каменной Вознесения Христова и с колокольнею весь розвалился, а теплой храм Покрова пречистые Богородицы в землю осел по нижние окошка.[87] А людей Бог измиловал, ни един человек не изгиб. А то все розломало ограду и ворота ‖ [л. 5 об.] монастырские и службы все. Бысть же сий трус при архимарите Трифоне. А[n] преже сего в том же Нижнем Новеграде за 400 лет была слобода вверх по Оке реке под старым городом,[о] и такоже опользла гора, яко и печерская, и зазыпало полтораста дворов с[88] людьми и со скотом, и ни един человек оттуду не избыл.

В лета 7104-го повеле государь, царь и великий князь Феодор Иванович всеа Русии в своей отчине в Казани в каменном нутри городе[89] в Преображенском монастыре каменную церковь заложити[90] боголепное Преображе- ‖ [л. 6] ние Господа нашего Исуса Христа. И начаша ров копати, и обретоша честныя мощи иже во святых отец наших Гурия архиепископа казанскаго и Варсунофия епископа тверскаго новых чюдотворцов октября в 4 день при митрополите казанском Ермогене и при архимарите Арсении Высоком.[85] ‖ [л. 7] Лета 7105-го июня в 12 день заложен бысть в Смоленску град каменной а окладывал его по государеву, цареву и великого князя Федора Ивановича всеа Русии веленью[91] шурин его, боярин и конюшей Борис Федорович Годунов.[92]

---

[n] In the margin in cinnabar and the same hand is written at this point зри.

[о] Corrected from A; in M горододом.

[83-83] This entry follows the next one in A.   [84] A adds белой.   [85-85] Omitted in second redaction (P).   [86] A adds холодной.   [87] окошко A.   [88] и A.
[89] города A.   [90] заложили A.   [91] Omitted P.   [92] Годонув A; added in second redaction (P): В лета 7092-го приходили крымские и нагайские люди 40,000, а с ними Араслан мурза Дивиев сын з братьею, и по грехом Оку реку перешли, и Козелеск и Мещеск и Масалеск и можайских и дорогобужских земских мест захватили по Угре реке и были в государъской [зе]мле две недели, и полону безчисленно взяли, [к]нягини и боярыни многие поимали и де[тей] их, и пошли из государевы земли.

[И] мая в 7 день на праздник явльшагося знамения на небеси честнаго и животворящаго креста Господня. На реке на Оке, на перелазе Усть Высы реки выше Колуги верст з десять пришол на крымских и на нагайских людей государев, царев и великого князя Феодора Ивановича всеа Росии воевода Михаило Ондреевич Безнин, а с ним государевы выборные дворяне большие князь Ондрей Васильевич Трубецкой да князь Ондрей Дмитреевич Хилков и иные многие большие дворяне и городовых детей боярских и стрельцы государевы дворовые, з головами, з Григорьем Микулиным да с Ондреем Митковым, и крымских и нагайских людей многих побили и потопили, и Дивиева сына убили и языки многие поимали, и полону отполонили больши 70,000, и княгинь и боярынь и детей их и вся[ких людей] и к Москве пришол, дал Бог, здорово со в[семи] государевыми дворяны. А в те поры на М[оскве] посол литовской Лев Сопега.
Того же месяца маия в 22 день по грехом, чернь московская приступали к городу большему кремлю, и ворота Фроловские выбили и секли, и пушку большую,

Лета[93] 7106-го генваря в 7 день преставися царь и великий князь Федор Ивановичь московский и всеа Русии, [94]удобрение и самодержец государства Московъского, своея великия отчины, и многих государств обладатель,[94] в 13 лето государства его.[95] Яко солнце заиде в далныя страны и земли, свеща русийская угасе, и яко камень драгий адамант лице свое сокры, во гроб вселися и в земли затворися, свет померче, ‖ [л. 7 об.] и красный цвет християнъский увяде. И яко кипарис крепкий ис корени исторжеся и не остася отрасли ни мала от семени.[96]

Сия же патриарх Иов московский видев, и с митрополиты и архиепископы и со всем освященным вселенским собором, и государевы, царевы и великого князя большие бояре и дворяне и гости и народ всея земли виде,[97] яко в Московъском государстве царского сродника ни единаго несть, кому на Московском государстве царем быти, а во иноверныя[98] земли во орды царя а в варязи короля просити на государство не изволиша послати, сицевы ради вины имея[99] во уме ужасть[100] и страх в сердцы. Цари ‖ [л. 87]ᵖ убо бохмичи имеют скверную бусорманскую веру, а короли еллини, своим изволением от Бога отпадоша и благоверия отвергошася, имеют богомерскую латынъскую и люторскую ересь, дабы на Московском государстве будучи християнъские правые веры не исказили, и к своей прелести к бусорманской вере и к богомерской латынской ереси благоверных християн насильством не превратили. И били челом благоверному государеву, цареву и великого князя Федора Ивановича шурину, боярину и конюшемуᑫ Борису Федоровичю Годунову ‖ [л. 87 об.] чтобы Борис Федоровичь пожаловал, приял престол Московского и Владимирского и Казанскаго и Астороханъского царства и сдержал скипетр всеа Русии на государево, царево и великого князя Феодора Ивановича всеа Русии место. И Борис Федоровичь челобитья их не презрил и просил срока, дондеже государю, царю и великому князю Феодору Ивановичю блаженные памяти 40 дни преидет, и от царицы и великие княгини Ирины Федоровны, сестры своей, получить благословение.

Тое же зимы царя и великого князя Феодора Ивановича царица Ирина пострижеся на Москве в пречестнем девечем монастыре пречистые Богородицы честнаго ея Одегитре и нареченна бяше Александра.

В лета 7107 сентября в 3 день по повелению царицы и великия княгиниᵖ ‖ [л. 8] иноки Александры и по благословению и челобитью святейшаго Иова патриарха московъского и по челобитью же всего освященнаго вселенъскаго собора и царевых и великого князя бояр и дворян и всего

ᵖ⁻ᵖ Text from *A*; omitted in *M*.　　ᑫ Corrected later from кошему.

которая стояла против Фроловских ворот на Лобном месте под город подворотили, и дети боярские многие на конех из луков на огрод стреляли. И в малые во Фроловские воротца выходили ко всей черни думной дворянин Михаило Ондреевичь Безнин да дьяк Ондрей Шелкалов, и чернь уговорили и с мосту сослали. При том же после литовском Льве тово же дни посол был у государя с утра.

⁹³ В лето *P*.　　⁹⁴⁻⁹⁴ Omitted *P*.　　⁹⁵ своего *P*; *P* adds [В л]ета 7107-го сентября в 3 день восприят скипетр [Москов]ского государства и многих государств всеа [Русии] Борис Федоровичь Годунов. The second redaction (*P*) ends with that line.
⁹⁶ *A* adds его.　　⁹⁷ видевше *A*.　　⁹⁸ инои верныя *A*.　　⁹⁹ имеяху *A*.
¹⁰⁰ ужас *A*.

воинъства и гостей и християнства поставлен бысть на Москве Богом избранный государь, царь и великий князь Борис Федоровичь на превелицем престоле царства Московъскаго, и благословением и рукоположением святейшаго Иова патриарха московскаго и вселенского венчан венцем царским и помазан святым миром.

И при его державе по вражью действу а по злому умышленью и по ненависти полского и литовского Жигимонта короля и панов рад ‖ [л. 8 об.] через многое его королевское крестное целованье в Московъском государстве смута и межусобье учинилася. Некоторой вор, чернец, еретик имянем Гришка Отрепьев,[101] за некоторые богомерские его дела, с Москвы збежал[102] в Литву, и свергл с себя черное платье, назвался царевичем Дмитреем углецким, великого государя, царя Ивана Васильевича всеа Русии сыном. А царевича Дмитрея не стало до того времени за 13 лет. И вражьим действом, тот вор Гришка дошел до царствующаго града Москвы и царского престола достиже, и государем московским именовася. И видя его злую прелесть, Московского государства бояре и всяких чинов люди сьехався изо всех государств в царствующий град Москву, и соединяся единомысленно и облича того вора, злой смерти предали. ‖ [л. 9]

И по убийстве того вора Гришки, по избранию всяких чинов и всего Российского государства учинился на Московском государстве государем, царем из бояр от рода суждальских князей Василей Ивановичь Шуйской. И после того Жигимонт король умысля Московское государство смутити больши прежнего. И поруша перемирье, и преступив свое ᵣкрестное целование, и после пословᵣ своих, которые учинили на Москве мир с царем Васильем иˢ крестное целованье. Наслал другово вора родом жидовина, назвав его царевичем Дмитреем же, будто он тот Гришка, что был на Москве и с Москвы убежалᵗ к ним в Польшу жив. И тот другой вор собрався, с литовскими людьми ‖ [л. 9 об.] пришед, под Москвою стоял таборами, и городы и уезды воевал, и кровь напрасную проливал, и к Москве приступал. А польской Жигимонт король через крестное целованье город Смоленск взяв, и умысля с ызменники Московского государства, сᵐ¹⁰³ Михаилом Глебовым Салтыковым и с его советники, которые изменили царю Василью, отехали х королю, писал и приказывал в Москву к бояром и всяких чинов к людем, бутто он, жалеючи о христианстве пришел в Московское государство, чтоб государство успокоить и кровь уняти, а быти б на Московском государстве сыну его коро- ‖ [л. 10] левичю Владиславу в нашей вере греческаго закона и никоторого зла в Московском государстве не делати. И царь Василей, для покою християнского, государство свое отставил. А на Московское государство избрали были польского королевича Владислава и з гетманом корунным с Станиславом Желковъским, и о том о всем договор был учинен, и крестным целованьем с обе стороны укреплен. И Жигимонт король сына своего на Московское государство не дал, и сам от Смоленска не

ᵣ⁻ᵣ Corrected from *A*; in *M* и послов.   ˢ Corrected from *A*; omitted in *M*.
ᵗ Repeated, the second time having been crossed out.

---

¹⁰¹ Отрепьет *A*.   ¹⁰² безжал *A*.   ¹⁰³ и *A*.

отшед,[104] и по его веленью литовские люди и изменник Михайло оманом вошли в Москву. И царя Василья взяв, х королю отослали, а Москву велел ‖ [л. 10 об.] польским и литовским людем выжечь и высечь, и церкви Божии и монастыри осквернили. И святейшаго Гермогена, патриарха московскаго и всеа Русии, с престола свергли и в заточенье уморили и всяких чинов людей множество побили и Москву засели. И Московского государства бояре и всякие люди, за ту[105] его королевъскую многую неправду, против его стали, и стоя под Москвою гетмана Карла Хоткеева побили, и з запасы в Москву не пропустили, и Московское[u] государство очистили. И на великих государствах, на Владимерском и Московском и Ноугородцком и на царствах Казанском и Астороханском и Сибирском и на всех великих ‖ [л. 11] и преславных государствах Российскаго царствия по Божией воли и по племени великих государей, царей российских а по благословению матерню великие государыни старицы иноко Марфы Ивановны и по избранию и по челобитью Московского государства царей и царевичев, которые служат в Московском государстве и бояр и окольничих и дворян[106] и всего Московского государства учинился государем, царем и великим князем Михаило Федоровичь всеа Русии самодержцем[107] в лето 7121-е, понеже он государь великого государя славные памяти царя и великого князя Ивана Васильевича всеа Русии самодержца[108] законные супруги а сына его царя и великого князя Федора Ивановича всеа Русии[109] ‖ [л. 11 об.] матери великие государыни[110] царицы и великие княгини Анастасей Романовны Юрьева родного племянника Федора Микитича Романова Юрьева сын.

Лета 7153-го году июля[111] против 13-го числа в ночи волею Божиею великого государя, царя и великого князя Михаила Федоровича всеа Русии самодержца не стало, оставя земное царства, отиде в вечное блаженство небеснаго царствия, а отходя сего света, великий государь, царь и великий князь Михаило Федоровичь всеа Русии благословил сына своего великого государя, [v]царевича князя[v] Алексея Михаиловича быти на своем царском престоле на Влади- ‖ [л. 12] мерском и на Московском государстве и на всех великих государствах Российскаго царствия царем и великим князем всеа Русии.

THE TALE OF THE NIZHNY NOVGOROD EARTHQUAKE

GPB, Collection of M. P. Pogodin, No. 1573

[л. 17] Печерский трус бысть в Нижном Новеград[е при][a] благочестивом царе и государе и великом князе Ф[едоре] Ивановиче всеа Русии в лето 7105-го [июня] в 18 день в третий час нощи. От монастыря к конюш[ен]ному двору и в монастырьскую слободку вверх по Волге реке, и на

---

[u] Corrected from московсковъское.   [v–v] Written above the line.

[a] Here and in other places indicated by brackets the text has been restored, since the corner of the manuscript has been torn off.

---

[104] отшел A.   [105] ту A.   [106] дворяв A.   [107] самодержец A.   [108] саморжца A.
[109] A adds самодержца.   [110] Omitted A.   [111] июня A.

монастыре и ниже монастыря до печер, вниз по Волге реке всего на версту появилися щели великия. И на всех пришел страх и ужас великой, яко же бысть преж сего по летописцем за четыриста лет. В Нижнем Новеграде под старым городом вверх по Оке реке была слобода, и Божий гнев в те лета были знамения такова: опользла гора сверху и засыпало полтораста дворов с людьми и со скотом, оттуду никаков человек не избыл. Тако же ныне в наша лета, грех ради наших, вся таковая страждем праведным судом, монастырь стоял в полу горе под большою горою, и почала большая гора под монастырем осыпатися и с лесом. Архимарит же || [л. 17 об.] [Трифон] з братьею и весь освященный собор нача [моли]ти милостиваго Бога, дабы укротил пра[ведн]ый свой гнев, и взем пречистыя Богородицы [об]раз и прочия чюдотворныя иконы, вышли за монастырь с плачем и с песньми духовными. И противо большие горы нача быти шум великой и треск от лесу, и Божиим милосердием и пречистыя Богородицы заступлением тоя милостию, прошла гора под монастырь под землею, и обявилася гора та в Волге реке. А которые суды были у брегу, и те стали на горе от воды далече, а в Волге учинилися бугры великия. И на монастыре и в слободе землю изломало, и монастырское основание все здвигнулося с места в Волгу реку, и храм большой каменной Вознесение Христово от того разрушилося до основания. Токмо остался един верх, которой был над жертвеником, и колокольница разсыпалася. А теплой храм Покров пресвятыя Богородицы сшатнуло на сторону и обнизился в землю || [л. 18] сажени с три блиско о конец олтарн[ы, святыя] ворота повалилися, и поварни и ледни[ки и су]шила, и хлебни и отграда монастырьское... строение переломало, и на брегу Волги хр[ам] Николы чюдотворца здвигнуло с места и паперть обломало, и в слободе дворы и[с]шатало. Аримарита же Трифона з братиею и монастырских слуг и християн от смерти Бог помиловал, ни един человек не изгибл, яко же и преж сего, грех ради наших, при царе Иустинияне бысть трус в Констянтине граде, по различных местех прият казнь.

Тако же и великий град Антиохия Божиим гневом напрасно весь падеся, и гроб бысть живущим в нем, инии же под землею падошася и погребошася, нецыи же живи суще, и огнь из земли пришед и пожре их, и тако же от аера огнь сходяи, яко молния, и последи обретающихся попаляющи. Понтийский же град разседеся на полы, пол его паде с живущими || [л. 18 об.]... под землею, взываху милости, прося... пребысть земля трясущися лето все.

THE BEZDNIN CHRONICLE

Text given according to MS GBL, *fond* 92, Collection of S. O. Dolgov, No. 3 (Museum Collection, No. 5890) (abbreviated *D*), with variants from MSS GIM, Collection of E. V. Barsov, No. 1811 (abbreviated *B*), and Museum Collection, No. 2524 (abbreviated *M*).

[л. 1] В лето 6463 крещение блаженные Ольги бабы великого князя Владимера.

В лето 6496 во царство Василья и Костятина греческих от патриярха Фотия крестися князь велики Владимер в Корсуни. И приведе с собою из грек перваго митрополита Леона в Киев и с ним 4 епископы, и крести русскую землю. И се бысть в Киеве первый митрополит Леон, а четырех епископов посадил по градом. Перваго посади в Белеграде и нарече архиепископом.[a] Втораго архиепископа посадил в Ростове; посла его с сыном своим со князем Борисом. Третьяго епископа посади в Чернигове. Четвертаго епископа посади в Волынской земли. Сей же митрополит Леон и сии 4 епископы крестиша рускую землю. Теи первопрестольницы нарицаются, якоже от сих нача || [л. 1 об.] множатися правоверная вера крестьяньская, и от Леона митрополита поставлени быша по иным градом епископы в Новград, в Полотеск, в Волынскую землю.

Ярослав, сын Владимеров,[112] постави в Новград перваго епископа Якима Волошенина. Тогда же и сына своего[b] старейшаго Владимера в Новеграде посади. Той же князь великий Ярослав постави по Акиме[113] втораго епископа Жидяту в Новеграде, нарицаемаго Луку.

В лето 6700 преставися преподобный игумен Варлам чюдотворец Футынский.[c]

В лето 6742 царь Батый приходил на Русь.

В лето 6754 убьение князя Михаила Черниговского и болярина его Феодора.

В лето 6791 поставлен бысть в митрополиты Максим гречанин. Жил || [л. 2] 22 лета.

В лето 6816 поставлен бысть в митрополиты Петр, и прииде в Володимер. Жил 20 лет в митрополитех.

В лето 6862 поставлен бысть во Цареграде Алексей митрополит, и[114] жил 23 лета, и положены бысть честныя его мощи в его созданней обители на Москве, в Чюдове монастыри в лето 885.

В лето 6879 родися князь Василей Дмитреевич Донскаго.

В лето 6888[d] побоище бысть великаго князя Дмитрея Ивановича Донскаго. Побил за Доном Момая царя.

В лето 6890 взял царь Тахтамыш град Москву оманом и много зла сотворил.

В лето 6897 преставися князь || [л. 2 об.] великий Дмитрей Иванович Донской месяца мая в 19 день.[115] Был на великом княжнение московском 29 лет и 6 месяц, а всех лет жил 38 и 5 месяць.

В лето 6898 преставися Пимин митрополит, что был по Алексее чюдотворце. Вооружился был на Олексеево место прияти престол митропольский Митяй, от Спаса с нового архимарит,[116] и мантию со источники на ся возложил самоволством. И пошел к Царюграду ститися, и Богу не попустившу ему таковаго престола святельска восприяти гордости ради.

В лето 6899[e] женился князь Василей Дмитреевич Донскаго. Понял Софию, дщерь Витовта Кестутевича, короля литовскаго. || [л. 3]

В лето 6900 преставися преподобный игумен Сергий чюдотворец

---

[a] Corrected from *B*; in *D* архиепископав. [b] Corrected from *B*; in *D* его. [c] *Sic.*
[d] Corrected from *B*; in D 6088. [e] Corrected from *B*; in *D* 6800.

---

[112] Владимир *B*. [113] Якиме *B*. [114] Omitted *B*. [115] Omitted *B*.
[116] архимандрит *B*.

радонежский. Того же году преставися преподобный игумен Дмитрий прилутцкий чюдотворец. Того же году окааный Темир Аксак приходил на Русь, и Елеч град взял, и князя елеческово полонил при благочестивом великом князе Василье Дмитреевиче Донскаго внука Ивана Ивановича а правнука Ивана Даниловича московскаго Калиты,[117] при митрополите Киприяне киевском и всеа Русии.

В лето 6903 прииде образ пречистые Богородицы из Володимера на Москву при великом князе Василье Дмитреевичя Донъскаго.

В лето 6904 преставися Стефан пермьский епископ на Москве || [л. 3 об.] и положен бысть у Спаса на государеве дворе.

В лето 6915 преставися великая княгиня[f] Евдокея княже Дмитреева Донского, во иноцех Ефросинья, месяца июня в 7 день. Она же идучи до манастыря Вознесенского к постриганью простила 30 человек, различными недуги одержимыя, а у князя Дмитреева гроба Донскаго в Архангиле на площади да у княгини Ефросинии в Вознесенском монастыре у гробов свещи сами о себе возгарахуся.

В лето 6916 поиде князь великий Василей Дмитреевич к Смоленску и взя град Дмитровец, и поиде к Вязме, и взяша с тестем своим с великим князем Витовтом перемирье от рожества святые Богородицы до Петрова дни.

Того же лета погоре град Ростов, и церковь || [л. 4] каменая соборная падеся, и колоколы разлишася, и людей много погоре и истопе месяца июня в 21 день.

В лето 6917 приде князь великий Витовт на зятя своего, на великого князя Василья Дмитреевича московского, и то слышав, князь великий Василей поиде противу его. И снидошася о реце о Угре и ту взяша мир промеж собою, занеже нелзе было снитися войском о том месте, дуброва частая и путь узок, и разыдошася.

На ту же зиму поиде безбожный князь Едигей на великого князя Василья Дмитреевича, идучи к Москве сожже град Серпухов, а людей множество ссече, а иных в полон поведе, и прииде к Москве декабря в 5 день, и земле русской много зла сътворил, || [л. 4 об.] а граду Москве ничтоже успе.

В лето 6918 выиде преосвященный митрополит Фотий киевский из Царяграда на Москву и на всю рускую землю, [118]и прииде на Москву[118] в Велик день, апреля в 22 день.

В лето 6930 глад бысть силен по всей русской земли, на Москве оков ржи [g]по рублю а Коломне оков ржи[g] по два рубля.[h]

В лето 6935 мор бысть силен на люди на Москве и по всей земли руской. Того же году преставися Кирил чюдотворец.

В лето 6936 преставися игумен Никон троецкий, Сергеев ученик, ноября в 17 день.

В лето 6938 съезд был в Литве к королю Витовту Кестутевичю, от многих земль великие князи и короли, митрополиты и владыки от

---

[f] Corrected from княгини. [g-g] Corrected from B; omitted in D. [h] Corrected from B; in D рубли.

[117] B adds и. [118-118] Omitted B.

различных || [л. 5] земль, послы и воеводы и князи местнии, и множество панов и боляр от многих царств, и многие гости и много безчислено людства. Первой был внук его князь великий Василей Васильевич московской, второй Гаило Олгирдович, король великополский, третей князь великий Борис Александрович тверский, четвертой Уныштер, великий воевода немецкий, пятой ардинал, посол от папы из Рима, шестой и семои[i] Лияшь да Стефан, воеводы волошские, осмой король чешьский, девятый Фотий, митрополит московский, десятой арцыбискуп краковский, первой на десять бискуп виленский, второй на десять бискуп полоцкий, князи местнии, бояре и панове || [л. 5 об.] и гости великие от различных стран. Князь же великий Витовт Кестутевич, почтив великими честьми и дары, и здарив коегождо по достоянию, и кормы посылая наряднье[119] по выписем, и учрежение велие творя по вся дни, и урядив всех о которых потребах сьехалися, отпусти с миром коегождо во свояси с великою честию, и в своей земли литовской по всем станом повелел събирати кормы великие, дондеже кождо их во свою землю прииде.

В лето 6939 преставися Фотий митрополит. Того же лета мгла стояла 6 недель, рыбы в воде мерли, тако же и птицы на землю падали, не видели летати. Того же году марта в 14 день преста- || [л. 6] вися игумен Христофор, Кирилов ученик.

В лето 6946 бой был на Белеве с великим князем Васильем Васильевичем царю Амету, и великого князя обили.

В лето 6948 родися князь велики Иван от великого князя Василья Васильевича.

В лето 6953 [120]бысть бой[120] под Суждалем с татары и великого князя Василья в полон взяли.

В лето 6954 князь великий Василей Васильевич вышел от царя ис полону. Тоеже зимы князь Дмитрей Шемяка да князь Иван Ондреевич можайской великого князя Василья Васильевича поимали у Троицы в Сергиеве монастыре и очи у него выняли. И дали ему Вологду в кормленье в удел. || [л. 6 об.]

В лето 6961 турский царь взял Царьград.

В лето 6980 после рожества Христова явися звезда велика, от нея же луч долог велми. Тоеже зимы генваря явися звезда хвостата. Того же лета приходил царь Ахмут и Олексин выжег.

В лето 6985 преставися преподобный игумен Пафнотий боровъский мая в 1 день.

В лето 6986 князь великий Иван Васильевич взял Новъград.

Того же году зиме родися великому князю Ивану Васильевичю сын Иван от великие княгини тверянъки.

В лето 6987[j] марта в 25 день родися князь великий Василей Ивановичь московский и крестиша его у Троицы || [л. 7] в Сергиеве монастыре.

В лето 6990 октября в 6 день родися великому князю Ивану Васильевичю сын Дмитрий.

---

[i] *Sic.*   [j] Corrected from *B*; in *D* 6087.

---

[119] нарядные *B.*   [120-120] бой был *B.*

В лето 6992 родися великому князю Ивану Ивановичю сын Дмитрей а внук великому князю Ивану Васльевичю.

В лето 6994 сентября в 12 день князь велики Иван Васильевич взял Тверь.

В лето 6995 князь великий Иван Ивановичь взял Казань, и от себя посла на царство в Казань Магмедиямина царя.

Того же лета родися великому князю Ивану Васильевичю сын Семен.

В лето 6997 преставися Геронтей митрополит всеа Русии. || [л. 7 об.]

В лето 6998[121] преставися князь Иван Ивановичь всеа Русии.

Того же году родися великому князю Ивану Васильевичю сын Ондрей.

В лето 6999 собор был на Москве на наугороцких еретиков при великом князе Василье Ивановиче всеа Русии.

В лето 7013 июня в 24 день[122] царь казанский Магмедеми гостей руских иссек в Казани, и отложилъся от великого князя, а Михаила Кляпика[123] поимал.

В лето 7014 преставися князь великий Иван Васильевич всеа Русии самодержец, а был на великом княженье 43 лета, а всех лет живота его 66.

Тоеже осени сын его князь велики Василей Иванович женился 26 лет. || [л. 8] Поял Соломонею, дщерь Юрья Сабурова.

Того же году князь великий Василей послал брата своего князя Дмитрея углетцкаго да князя Федора Борисовича володцкаго под Казань а с ними множество воевод и воинства, и людей руских обили и запас отлучили.

В лето 7022 князь великий Василей Ивановичь взял у литовского короля град столный Смоленеск месяца июля.

Того же лета побили московских воевод в литовской земли под Оршею.

[124]В лето 7024 преставися преподобный игумен Иосиф волоцкий сентября в 9 день.[124]

В лето 7029 преставися князь Дмитрей Иванович углетцкой.

Того же лета обретоша мощи Макария чюдотворца колязинскаго месяца июня. || [л. 8 об.]

Того же лета июля в 26[125] приходил царь Магмет а силы с ним было 130 тысящь и много зла сотворил крестьянству.

В лето 7039 августа в 25 день[126] с середы на четверг родися великому князю Василью Ивановичю сын, и нарекоша имя ему Иван.

В лето 7042 преставися князь великий Василей Иванович самодержец всеа Русии. На государьстве был 28 лет, а всех лет жил 54 и 8 месяць и 9 дней.

В лето 7043 июля в 3 день родися благоверному князю Ондрею Ивановичю старитцкому сын Владимер.

В лето 7046 преставися благоверная великая княгиня Елена апреля в 3 день в 2 час дни. || [л. 9]

В лето 7048 апреля в 7 день в первый час тма была до четвертаго часа дни.[k]

---

[k] Added and crossed out и снег пал по многим местом.

---

[121] 6098 B.   [122] Omitted B.   [123] Кляпика B.   [124-124] Omitted B.
[125] B adds день.   [126] Omitted B.

В лето 7050 августа в 22 день студь была велика и снег пал по многим местом.

В лето 7061 царь и великий князь Иван Васильевич взял Царство казанское и обеих царей Семиона и Александра свел к Москве и учинил вся по своей воли, и воевод своих посадил и людей[1] многих воиньских оставил.

В лето 7068 преставися благоверная великая княгиня Анастасья августа в 7 день.

В лето 7071 царь и великий князь Иван Васильевич взял литовский столный град Полотеск.

В[127] лето[128] 7079[129] в приход крымского царя Девлет Кирея Москва вся погорела, а Москвы не взял, побежал Божиим || [л. 9 об.] гневом гоним. В той же пожар преставися князь Иван Дмитреевич Бельской з дыму и от великого пожару, а был ранен во многих местех от татар, месяца мая в 24.[130]

В лето[131] 7080[132] июля той[133] же царь крымский Девлет Кирей приходил на Русь с великою похвалою и хотел аки лев похитити[134] все царство Московское, и не чаял[135] окаанный злодей противу себе московские рати. И Бог человеколюбец и пречистая Богородица отврати гнев свой праведный от православнаго крестьянства и великие чюдотворцы руские[136] молитвою помогли, и от града Москвы царь побежал никем же гоним, и как будет на Молодях и государьские воеводы князь Михайло Иванович Воротынской с товарыщи да князь Иван Петрович Шуйской, царя крымского обили,[137] и большово воеводу Дивия мурзу взяли жива. || [л. 10]

В лето[138] 7090[139] преставися царевич князь Иван Иванович ноября в 19[140] в 13 час нощи а всех лет живота его 29 лет[m] и 7 месяц.

В лето[141] 7091 у царя и великого князя Ивана Васильевича всеа Русии родися сын и нарекоша имя ему царевичь Дмитрей, месяца октября в 19[142] на память святаго пророка Иоиля.

В лето[143] 7092[144] преставися царь и великий князь Иван Васильевич всеа Русии самодержец марта в 18 день с середы на четверг в пятом часу нощи, а всех лет живота его 53 лета и 7 месяц.

Того же году седе на царство на Москве сын его царевич князь Феодор Иванович[145] месяца мая в 31 день[146] в неделю 7 по Пасце[n] а от рожества его 28 лет.

Того же лета приходили крымские || [л. 10 об.] и нагайские люди[147] 40,000 Аросла[148] мурза Дивиев сын з братею, и по грехом Оку реку перелазили,[149] [150]и воевали многие городы за Окою рекою,[150] и Козелеск, и

---

[1] Corrected from *B*; in *D* люде.   [m] Corrected from *B*, *M*; omitted in *D*.
[n] Corrected from *B*, *M*; in *D* Пас.

---

[127] *M* begins here.   [128] лета *M*.   [129] 7079-го *M*.   [130] *B*, *M* add день.
[131] лета *M*.   [132] 7080-го *M*.   [133] тот *M*.   [134] восхитить *M*.   [135] чаяв *M*.
[136] московские *B*.   [137] отбили *M*.   [138] лета *M*.   [139] 7090-го *M*.
[140] *B*, *M* add день.   [141] лета *M*.   [142] *B*, *M* add день.   [143] лета *M*.
[144] 7092-го *M*.   [145] *M* adds всеа Русии самодержец руския земли и всея области.
[146] Omitted *B*.   [147] *M* adds а их.   [148] Араслан *M*.   [149] перешли *M*.
[150–150] Omitted *M*.

Мещовъск,[151] и Мосалеск, и можайских и дорогобужских [152]и вяземских[152] мест захватили по Угре по реке, и были в государьской земли 2 недели, и полону безчисленно взяли, и княгини и боярыни многие поимали и детей их, и пошли из государевы земли. И мая в 7 день[153] явльшагося знамение[154] на небеси честнаго и животворящаго креста Господня на реце на Оке на перелазе Усть Высы реки свыше[155] Колуги [156]десять верст.[156] Пришол на крымских и на нагайских людей государевь[157] воевода Михайло Ондреевич Бездрин, а с ним государевы выборные дворяне большие князь Ондрей Васильевич Трубетцкой да ‖ [л. 11] князь Ондрей[158] Дмитреевич Хилков, и иные многие большие дворяне, и городы[159] детей боярских, и стрельцы [160]дворовые государевы[160] з головами з Григорьем с Микулиным да с Ондреем с Митковым, да[161] крымских и нагайских людей многих побили [162]и потопили,[162] и Дивиева сына убили и языки многие поимали и полону отполонил боле[163] семидесят тысящь, и княгинь и боярынь и детей их[164] и к Москве пришел, дал Бог, здорово со всеми государевыми дворяны. А в те поры был[165] на Москве посол литовской Лев Сопега.

И[166] того же месяца в 22 день по грехом чернь московъская приступали к городу большому,[167] и ворота Фроловские выбивали[168] и секли, и пушку болшую, которая стояла[169] на Улобном[170] месте, на[171] город поворотили,[172] и дети боярские ‖ [л. 11 об.] многие на конех из луков на город стреляли.[173] В малые во Фроловские воротца выходили ко всей черни думной дворянин Михайло Ондреевич Бездрин да дияк Ондрей Щелкалов, и чернь уговорили и с мосту сослали при том же после литовском Льве. Того же дни посол был у государя с утра.[174]

В лето 7093 приехал царевич Мурат Кирий крымской, Девлет Киреев[175] сын, царю государю служити, Федору Ивановичю московъскому.

В лето 7094 приехал к Москве патриарх антиохийский Иоаким, а в Чюдове хлеба ял месяца июля в 16 день в воскресный день.

---

[151] Мещеск M; Мещевъск B.   [152-152] земских M.   [153] M adds на праздник.
[154] знамения M.   [155] выше M.   [156-156] версть з десять M.   [157] M adds
царев и великого князя Феодора Ивановича всеа Русии.   [158] он B.
[159] городовых M.   [160-160] государевы дворовые M.   [161] и M.   [162-162] Omitted B.
[163] больши M.   [164] M adds и всяких людей.   [165] Omitted M.   [166] Omitted M.
[167] M adds х кремлю.   [168] выбили M.   [169] M adds против Фроловских ворот.
[170] Лобном M.   [171] под M.   [172] подворотили M.   [173] M, B add и.
[174] M ends at this point.   [175] Киев B.

Doctor Christopher Reitinger and a Seal of Tsar Boris Godunov

By JOHN H. APPLEBY

In July 1763 the following letter appeared in the *Gentleman's Magazine*:

Mr. Urban

Upon a brass plate inserted in a stone in the isle of *Newington* church, about three miles distant from *Hithe* in *Kent*, is the following inscription:

'*Doct.* Christopher Reitingerus, *natione Hungarus, Professione Medicus, per Septennium Archiatros, Imperatori* Russiae, Muscovi, etc. *Potentissimo. Sepultus fuit in hac Ecclesia Trices Die Mensis* Decembris 1612. *Aetatis Sue* 55.'

There is also an entry in the parish register of this person, written also in *Latin*, and corresponding exactly with this inscription, except that the word *Potentissimo* is wanting, *suae* also is falsely spelt *sue*.

Of this *Christopher Reitinger*, though principal physician to the Emperor of *Russia*, we may, perhaps, justly say with respect to his place of interment, what *Pope* says of the insects that are sometimes found in amber,

> *The things themselves are neither choice nor rare,*
> *We wonder how the Devil they came there.*

If any of your numerous correspondents can recollect any incident that will account for this phaenomenon, and will communicate it to the publick by your Magazine, they will oblige several of your readers, particularly *Yours*, &c. J. H.[1]

Not surprisingly, perhaps, no reader was able to shed any light on the subject.

Today, however, there are several sources of information which help to remove some of the obscurity surrounding Dr Christopher Reitinger.

The first that is heard of him is when he accompanied Sir Richard Lee on his embassy to Russia (July 1600 to April 1601).[2] Before he left Moscow, Lee petitioned Boris Godunov to take into his service, as doctor, one Christopher Reitinger, whom he highly recommended as a man who had skilfully tended Lee himself over the past twenty-six years, i.e. since 1575. From the evidence of his epitaph it would then appear that Reitinger was only 18 years old when first employed by Lee, and it was not until 19 October 1594 that he was licensed to practise as

---

[1] *Gentleman's Magazine*, xxxiii (1763), 340. The brass plate referred to in the letter is still in Newington church, now on the south wall of the nave (information kindly supplied by Mr Michael Jack, churchwarden of St. Nicholas's Church, Newington-next-Hythe).

[2] For Lee's mission to Russia, see T. S. Willan, *The Early History of the Russia Company, 1553–1603* (Manchester, 1956), 233–6, and N. Evans, 'Queen Elizabeth I and Tsar Boris: Five Letters, 1597–1603', *Oxford Slavonic Papers*, xii (1965), 49–68.

a physician and surgeon at Canterbury with the title 'A.P.P. (artis phisice professor)'.[3]

That Christopher Reitinger soon justified his appointment was remarked by John Merrick, who delivered Boris Godunov's letter of 12 June 1602 to Queen Elizabeth at Oatlands, near London, on 5 September that year.[4] Merrick, who had been received in audience by Boris Godunov in Moscow on 11 February 1602, writes:

> Further the Emperor tooke occasion to speake of doctor Christopher the Hungarian who went out with Sir Richard Lea, and said he was much beholding to her Majestie for him, and willed me that I should not forgeat to give her Majestie great thanks for him, for he had cured him of a dangerous sicknes: And the said Doctor acknowledgeth the Queen's Majestie to be his onlie soveraigne, and none other.[5]

One can only speculate on the nature of this illness, which, as will be seen, occurred in July or August 1601—only a few months after Sir Richard Lee's departure. Reitinger himself modestly mentions it in a letter to Sir Robert Cecil, Secretary of State, delivered by Merrick and summarized among the Salisbury Papers as follows:

> Although it has pleased God to place him here in a station far beyond his strength and sufficiency (and what assistance God gave him therein he refers to the Emperor's gracious letters testimonial), yet he will never neglect his duty to her Majesty, and will perform any service for her or for the public good that Cecil may enjoin him to. There is no potentate in the world that more highly esteems and more affectionately regards the Queen than this mighty monarch of all Russia; and being the like assured from her Majesty, the Emperor was the more willing to make choice of him to succeed his late deceased physician. If Cecil will make her Majesty acquainted therewith, he doubt not but that it will be sufficient excuse for any fault by him unwittingly committed, and that she will recall him and deliver him out of the golden fetters he is here bound in, to enjoy once again the sight of so precious a jewel, etc.—From this great city of Mosco, last of May, 1602.[6]

Richter, in his history of Russian medicine, refers to two contemporary sources which reveal more about Christopher Reitinger. Conrad Bussow, who knew him personally, reported that he was a remarkable man and fluent in many languages, while Petreius stresses that he was the most eminent of Godunov's five doctors and appointed 'archiater' because of his superior skill and experience.[7]

---

[3] Canterbury Cathedral Archives, Library and City Record Office, 'General Licences for Canterbury Diocese', vol. iv, f. 60. I should like to record my gratitude to the Archivist, Miss A. M. Oakley.   [4] Bodleian MS, Ashmole 1538.

[5] BL Cotton MS, Nero B.VIII, f. 39.

[6] Historical Manuscripts Commission, *Calendar of the Manuscripts of the Marquis of Salisbury*, xii (1910), 172.

[7] W. von Richter, *Geschichte der Medicin in Rußland*, i (Moscow, 1813), 372–4. For Bussow, see the recent edition, *Moskovskaya khronika* (M.–L., 1961), 85; for Petreius, see *Chteniya v Obshchestve istorii i drevnostei rossiiskikh*, 1866, i, 166.

Russian medical historians tell us virtually nothing about Boris Godunov's court physicians. An intriguing sidelight is thrown on them, however, by the illness and death of Prince John, son of King Christian IV of Denmark, in Moscow in 1602. Godunov had sought to forge a Russo-Danish alliance by marrying his daughter Xenia to Prince John, who arrived in the Russian capital on 19 September 1602 with the Danish ambassador Axel Gueldenstern and a large entourage, including two doctors. Prince John was taken ill with a high fever on 15 October and died thirteen days later. According to Levesque,[8] Godunov sent all his own physicians to try to save the Prince's life, and when they failed they had to hide until his wrath had cooled.[9]

On 7 November 1602 another Canterbury man, the apothecary James Frencham, arrived in Moscow with his wife and children. This was his second visit to Russia, for he had earlier established the first court pharmacy in 1581, returning to England in May 1583 with Sir Jerome Bowes. In 1585 Frencham, described as a merchant and the son of Dunstan Frencham, a tailor, had been made a freeman by birth of the City of Canterbury;[10] he had become a member of the Common Council in 1591 and an alderman in 1592.[11] Sir Richard Lee (who had acquired the manor of Dungeon, or Dane John, on the outskirts of Canterbury in 1589)[12] had asked Godunov, in a letter of 1 June 1602, to continue his favours to Dr Reitinger, '. . . and that it would please your Majestie to grace with your Princely fauore James Frencham, whoe this yeare in his much affection to serue your Majestie is retourned to your Majesties seruice of an apoticarie . . .'.[13] Frencham this time brought with him a large and valuable supply of medicines and a recommendatory letter from Elizabeth, dated 11 March 1602, in which the Queen pointed out that Frencham's services had been requested both 'by mocion made by Your Highnes Chaunccellor unto our late Ambassador Sir Michail Lea Knight, as by Your Majestis owne Ambassador also', and assured Godunov that 'hee is a man very skylfull in his profession and for his honesty hath byn employed under us in a office of good reputation and trust'.[14]

Evidently, Christopher Reitinger had contemplated remaining in Russia for only a short period, for on 10 April 1604 he again wrote to Sir Robert Cecil:

[8] Pierre-Charles Levesque, *Histoire de Russie* (Paris, 1782), ii, 214.
[9] Richter, op. cit. (n. 7), 402–9.
[10] J. M. Cowper, *The Roll of the Freemen of the City of Canterbury* (Canterbury, 1903), cols. 35, 200. Also a letter from Dr T. D. Whittet, chairman of the Faculty of the History of Medicine and Pharmacy, of the Worshipful Society of Apothecaries of London.
[11] Letter from the Archivist, Canterbury Cathedral Archives, Library and City Record Office.
[12] E. K. Chambers, *Sir Henry Lee* (Oxford, 1936), 177.
[13] *Sbornik Imperatorskogo russkogo istoricheskogo obshchestva*, xxxviii (1883), 416.
[14] Richter, op. cit. (n. 7), 396–401, 448–55.

The Seal of Boris Godunov (*diameter* 26·5 cm.)
Reproduced by permission of the Ashmolean Museum

In my last letter, delivered by Mr. Merick, being then physician to Sir Richard Lea, the Queen's ambassador to the Emperor, I was your suitor that after some labour in my art I might be recalled to England, my exopted haven in this worldly pilgrimage through your mediation. Owing to the Queen's death [on 24 March 1603] I was forced to attend with a more convenient time to renew my suit. Which being come with the rising of this pleasant morning sun, I crave my petition to take place.[15]

This letter crossed with one written to Godunov on 30 May 1603 by King James I:

Ryght high excellent Lord, We have for some causes greate desire to use the advise of one doctor Christopher Reytingher a physician whome we understand to be in your service and whose skill may serve us to good purpose in that wherin he can practice as we are informed above other men. Wherefore although sins our coming to this our crown of England, there hath not yet passed anie other matter of embassy between us yet are we glad that we have occasion to [?] bargaine with you being mynded to continew towards you all our good will which we understand was between the Queen our sister, deceased, and you, in confydence whereof we pray you to give leave to the said doctor Christopher R. to repaire unto us for a tyme whom we will as willingly license to return to you when we have had use of him in such things as we desire to use his service in. And will take it in very kinde and thankfull part to obtain our request of you.[16]

Sir Thomas Smythe, England's special ambassador to Russia, reached Archangel on 22 July 1604. He was second surviving son of Thomas Smythe of Ostenhanger (now Westenhanger) in Kent, and his grandfather, Sir Andrew Judd, was one of the founders of the Muscovy Company.[17] Soon after his arrival in Russia Smythe wrote the following letter to Sir John Leveson Sr., of Halling, Kent (*fl. c.* 1586–1614), who was the heir of Admiral Sir Richard Leveson and a Deputy Lieutenant for the County of Kent from 1590—reminding us, once again, of the strong Kentish links with Russia at this period.

Sir,
Beinge safly ariued at the port of St. Michels in Muscovy I haue thought good to discharge the trust committed vnto me by you, tochinge the pearle I receued from you I vnderstand ther is littell sale for them at this place but I am put in hope that I shall sell them at the Musco at your owne price at the least which I will do rather then I will returne them agane into England accordinge to your desire: but beinge rated at 10s they are not worth the adventure hether. I haue also inquired of the samples you gaue me, and do find that if they weare bored they would yeald the prises you set vpon them,

---

[15] Op. cit. (n. 6), xvi (1933), 54.
[16] PRO, S.P. 91/1, f. 193. My thanks are due to Mr Norman Evans for the transcription.
[17] *DNB*, s.v. 'Smith'. Smythe was Governor of the East India Company in 1600 and 1603–21.

excepe those of 40ts [*sic*], which will not yeald aboue 30s: wherefore if you desire to be ride of them I do thincke it your best waye to cause them to be bored and to send them hether directed to me the next yeare (if I be not come into England before) and I receuinge the same wilbecom your debtor at the rates you set downe so that those of 40s be rated at 30s which is all they will yeald for any thinge I heare, or else, if you thinke not well of that, you may leaue them of 40s vnsent, if you can make more then 30s ther in England. If you resolue heare of, they must be redie to be deliuered to this bearer my sarvant by the ende of Aprill, that they may be sent me by the first shipes for that my meaning is to retourne presently after ther comminge hether, so that if they be not com hether befor my returne I shall not take any good order for them. You shall heare of my man ether at Nettelsted [Nettlestead], about 4 miles south-west of Maidstone, Kent or at Mr. Crispes house in Grahons [Gracechurch?] streat in London from time to time. I have heare with sent you the samples againe because you may the better deserne of them, and haue also kept some of euery one because I would make further inquiry of them for the better sale thereof if they come. Thus with my very kinde comendations to you and your good lady I leaue you to the blessed protection of the Almightie from the Arkeangell this 6th of August 1604

Your very louinge and assured frend

Tho: Smythe

[Addressed]: To the Right Worshipfull his very louinge frend Sir Jhon [*sic*] Lewson Knight at his house neare Rochester in Kent.[18]

Sir Thomas Smythe met Christopher Reitinger, as the anonymously written account of his embassy relates:

The *Ambassador* kept here a great Christmas [1604/5] hauing a good company, not without some sports befitting his state, and the present time.

Vpon New-yeeres day, he was very honourably presented with New yeers-gifts, from master Doct. *Christopher Writtinger*, the *Emperors* chiefe *Physitian*, some of the *Kinges* Gentlemen, Maister *Iohn Mericke* and his wife, and many other *English Marchaunts*. . . .[19]

Boris Godunov's death on 13 April 1605 is also described by the same writer:

Here it might be befitting this my relation, to declare somwhat at large the *Emp.* death, the cause or disease. . . . His death was very suddaine, and as it was in it selfe, verye straunge: for within some two houres after dinner hauinge (as hee vsuallie had) his Doctors with him, who lefte him in theyr Iudgements in health, as the good meale hee made could witnes, for he dined well, and fed plentifully, though presently after as may be thought, feeding ouer much, he felt himselfe not onely heauy, but also pained in his

---

[18] Staffordshire Record Office, D. 593/S/4/69/19, Sutherland Papers, four sheets. This letter was found among Lieutenancy papers at Dunrobin Castle, but appears to have strayed from Sir John Leveson's personal correspondence (letter from Dr M. O'Sullivan, Assistant Archivist).

[19] *Sir Thomas Smithes Voiage and Entertainment in Rushia* (London, 1605), f. F4ʳ.

stomacke: presently went into his chamber, laid himself vppon his bed, sent for his Doctors (which alwaies speeded) yet before they came, he was past, being speechles and soone after dying . . . .[20]

In view of the circumstances of Godunov's death and the ensuing turbulent events of the Time of Troubles, it seems more than likely that Christopher Reitinger left Russia very soon afterwards, possibly returning to England with Sir Thomas Smythe, who sailed from Archangel in May 1605, or travelling overland via Hungary, his native country. However that may be, he is next documented in England: a bond, dated 3 November 1607 and witnessed by Tho. Flemyng, pledges a London mercer, William Russell,[21] to pay £350 to 'Christopher Ritinger . . . de London in medecine professor'; three seals are attached to the parchment deed, one of which incorporates an eagle displayed surmounting an escutcheon. This coat of arms may have been Reitinger's own, since another bond, dated on the dorse 3 May 1609 and signed by Nicholas Sherborne, promises to repay £40 to 'Christoferro Reittinger, de London, *Armiger*'. On the face of this second bond is a further commitment by Sherborne to repay £20 by 4 November 1609 to Reitinger 'at the now dwelling-house of James Colbron in Walbrooke in London'.[22]

A probate inventory, as well as Christopher Reitinger's will, is held at the Kent County Archives, Maidstone. Entitled 'An Inventorie of the Goods & Chattels of Christopher Reittinger Doctor of Phisicke deceased', it was made on 13 March 1613. Since Reitinger was not a householder, the inventory is fairly brief, the total value of goods amounting to £165. 3s. The items include 'a Jewell of gould with rich stones' worth £50, a bond owed by Nicholas Sawkins (one of the executors of Reitinger's will), and unspecified books valued at £5.[23]

Of more significance is Christopher Reitinger's will, proved on 21 April 1613.[24] At the time of his death Reitinger was living in the manorhouse of a wealthy landowner, Henry Brockman of Beachborough, Newington-next-Hythe, who was married to Helen, daughter of the Nicholas Sawkins of Lyminge mentioned above.[25] Both Sawkins and

[20] Ibid. f. H2r–v.

[21] William Russell may be the man of that name 'sometimes Agent for the Dutch', who accompanied Sir Thomas Smythe and John Merrick from Moscow to 'Bratteshin' on 20 March 1605 (ibid. f. G4v).

[22] BL Add. Charters 70496 and 70498. These bonds and Add. Charter 70629 (a copy of Reitinger's will) are among the Brockman family documents which were deposited at the British Museum in the early 1930s.

[23] Maidstone, Kent County Archives Office, Cat. Mk. PRC LO/52/276, probate inventory. My acknowledgements are due to Dr Felix Hull, County Archivist.

[24] Ibid. Original will: PRC 16/148; registered copy: PRC 17/55/232; BL copy: Add. Charter 70629; there is also a photo-copy in the Bodleian Library: MS Facs. b. 18, ff. 131–4.

[25] E. Hasted, *The History and Topographical Survey of the County of Kent*, iii (Canterbury, 1790), 394–5, 398 (footnote).

Brockman were executors of the will in which Reitinger made several bequests to Brockman's family and servants. Reitinger leaves various items to Thomas Willes, apothecary of Dover, such as a 'syring serveing both mann and woman', 'my great Lattin Herball', and 'my brazenn mortar'. He obviously had numerous contacts with Canterbury, as he mentions several legatees and the 'Congregacon of Strangers' and the 'French congregation' there. Reitinger had stood godfather to the Vicar of Newington's son, and he left his copy of Flavius Josephus' *Antiquitates Judaicae* as a 'remembraunce to John Peive minister', and another gift to 'Mr. Peeter Lewes, minister of the worde of god of Burneham in Essex'. A further bequest to John Brooke of Hook Norton, Oxfordshire, doubtless dates back to an acquaintance made at the time when Richard Lee married, in about the year 1580, Mary, daughter of John Blundell of Finmere and Steeple Barton in Oxfordshire and widow of Sir Gerald Croker of Hook Norton.[26]

The most interesting legacy in Reitinger's will reads:

I give my lettere of recommendation with a seale of masee pure gold thereto annexed given to mee by the moste high and mightie greate duke of all Russia Borice Theodorowits for my true service and difficult cure I performed (next unto God) upon his bodye which is written in the Russian tounge, which I desire to have translated by Mr. Richard Finche merchaunte of London, a follower of Sir Thomas Smith Knight citizen of London, to which Mr. Finche I give for his paines the some of twentye shillinges, which lettere of commendacon with the seale of gold thereto belongeing I give unto the most renowned librarye created in Oxforde by Sir Thomas Bodley knight.

It was not until 1621—eight years after the probate—that the Bodleian Library's Register of Benefactors recorded the receipt of Christopher Reitinger's seal, letters testimonial, and fifteen books (one of which is dated 1622) purchased from the £10 which Reitinger also left to the Library.[27]

Along with miscellaneous objects, Reitinger's seal and letters testimonial were transferred to the Ashmolean Museum in the nineteenth century. The double-sided seal is, in fact, bronze-gilt and not gold. The letters testimonial originally attached to it are now missing, but fortunately a translation of their text was printed in 1672 by Elias Ashmole, Windsor Herald, in his work on the Order of the Garter.[28] In a section of the book devoted to the 'lesser George' Ashmole writes that other countries than England and some families, including the

---

[26] Chambers, op. cit. (n. 12), 175–6.
[27] Bodleian Library, 'First Register of Benefactors', ff. 233ᵛ–234.
[28] Elias Ashmole, *The Institutions, Laws and Ceremonies of the Most Noble Order of the Garter* (London, 1672), 229–30. An excellent engraving of the seal, signed 'W. Hollar' and dated '1667', faces p. 229.

Emperors of Russia, have chosen St. George as their patron. The relevant passage runs:

There is preserved in the Archives at *Oxford*, an Instrument containing Letters testimonial of this Emperor [Boris Godunov], given to Doctor *Christopher Ritinger* his chief Physician, the Seal whereof is Silver gilt . . . and contains on the reverse the Figure of St. George and the Dragon only. A translation of the whole Instrument I have transcribed hither, as it was communicated to me by my worthy friend Mr. *Thomas Hyde,* the present Library-Keeper of that famous *University,* a Gentleman of eminent Learning, in all kinds, and especially in the Oriental Tongues.

By the great mercy of God, *We, great Lord Emperor and great Duke* Borrys Feodorwich *of all* Russia . . . *together with our princely Son* Phedor Burrissiwich, *of all* Russia, *do by these our princely Letters, given unto Doctor* Christopher Ritinger *Physician,* Hungarian *born, acknowledge his true, faithful, and willing service unto our Highness: in which his profession, We lord, King and Great Duke* Burrys Feodorwich *of all* Russia, *have sufficiently tryed his skill, on our princely person, which he carefully performed for the better preservation of our health: and through Gods great mercy, by his diligent and faithful service hath cured our Highness of a dangerous sickness. And therefore we Lord King and great Duke* Borys Feodorwich *of all* Russia *sole Commander, with our princely Son* Pheodor Burryssiwich, *in regard of his great learning and faithful service to us, have admitted him to be our Princely Doctor, to minister Physick, and attend on our royal person: to which end we have granted him our Letters, and hereby we testifie his sufficient knowledge and practice in Physick, who hath by our selves well deserved, to publish and make known the same. And if the said Doctor* Christopher *shall repair to any other* Princes, Countries, Emperors, Kings, Curfists, Arch-Dukes *or* Dukes, *to offer his service unto them, We do by these our princely Letters wheresoever they shall come, give true testimony on the said Doctor* Christopher*'s behalf, to be of great learning, sufficient knowledge, well practised in Physick matters: as also in that profession, careful, diligent, and trusty to be credited, We having had sufficient tryal of his faithful carriage, in all true and honest services towards us. These our Princely Letters given in our great and chiefest* Palace *in the Kingdom of* Mosco, *in the year of the creation of the* World 7109 [1601] *and in the moneth of August.*

The Style about the Seal.

By the great mercy of God, We great Lord, Emperor, and great Duke Borys Feodorwich *of all* Russia *sole Commander, Lord and Governor of many other Countries and* Kingdoms.

As our plate shows, the seal is a fine impression of Boris Godunov's small (or *kormlenaya*) seal,[29] which happily serves to link the Ashmolean Museum in Oxford with seventeenth-century Muscovy through the persons of a Hungarian physician, a Kentish diplomat, and a group of Kentish Muscovy merchants.

[29] E. I. Kamentseva and N. V. Ustyugov, *Russkaya sfragistika i geral'dika* (M., 1974), 129–30.

Yakov Smirnov and the Law of Nations

By W. E. BUTLER

THE enactment by Parliament in 1709 of an Act regulating more precisely the privileges and immunities of foreign diplomats in Great Britain in consequence of an affront to the Russian Ambassador, A. Matveev, who was arrested in connection with a private lawsuit, was a landmark in the development of the law of nations for which other Russian diplomatic agents had reason to be grateful.[1] One of these was Ya. I. Smirnov (1754–1840), whose remarkable role in Anglo-Russian relations has already been sketched in these pages,[2] but whose part in an escapade which raised questions of diplomatic immunity has not hitherto been known. In addition to offering more insight into Smirnov's character and activities, the episode also tells us something of the late eighteenth-century state practices relating to the right of chapel and to the immunities enjoyed by the Russian ambassador's retinue.

I

On Sunday morning, 10 April 1796, the Revd Smirnov was diverted from his usual clerical preoccupations as chaplain to the Russian Embassy by the necessity of laying before the Russian Ambassador, Count S. R. Vorontsov (1744–1832), the details of a 'disagreeable Transaction' which had taken place at Smirnov's house the preceding evening. Having returned from his visit to Vorontsov in the afternoon of 9 April, Smirnov passed the evening at a friend's house, where at about 10 p.m. his younger brother Ivan arrived to inform him that three individuals were waiting at his home, in 50 Upper Marylebone Street, to seize his goods in satisfaction of a debt. Smirnov took leave of his host and upon returning home found a young lad of 15 or 16 years, being assisted by an older man, there to take the goods in satisfaction of a debt of £16. 5s. 9d. under the supervision of a Mr Thompson, 'Officer to the Palace Court'.

In the encounter which ensued the chaplain at once asserted the immunity of his premises and property:

I beg to inform you Sir, that the House in which you are now, belongs to the Embassy of Her Imperial Majesty the Empress of all the Russias; that I had

---

[1] See W. E. Butler, 'Anglo-Russian Diplomacy and the Law of Nations' in: A. G. Cross (ed.), *Britain and Russia: Contacts and Comparisons, 1700–1800* (Newtonville, Mass., 1978).

[2] A. G. Cross, 'Yakov Smirnov: a Russian Priest of Many Parts', *Oxford Slavonic Papers*, NS, viii (1975).

the honour to belong to the same; that I was protected by His Excellency
the Russian Embassador . . . and as a Proof of my being protected, he might
see my name at the Secretary of State's Office and in all other offices proper
for it.[3]

According to Smirnov, Thompson claimed to have knowledge of all
this and of the 'Laws of his Country, which the Embassador cannot be
supposed to know so well . . .'. Smirnov said he would not interrupt the
proceedings, but sent his brother, who was present during the exchange,
to Vorontsov. Ivan Smirnov returned with the ambassador's response
'that I should not interrupt their Proceedings, and that your Excellency
was certain of obtaining every satisfaction due to the Rights [Law] of
Nations and to Her Imperial Majesty's Mission'.[4] Thompson decided
at that point, since it was nearly 1 a.m. on Sunday, to defer his business
until the following Monday. Smirnov retained the writ served on him,
which he attached to his letter to Vorontsov, noting that it was signed
for the Court by one H. F. Campbell and witnessed by Sir James Bland
Burges, Bt.; that the plaintiff was Andrew Gale; and that Gale was
represented by a solicitor named Heighway.

He also took special care to inquire whether Sir James B. Burges
(1752–1824) was personally acquainted with the transaction. Thompson
believed not. Smirnov doubtless suspected this was the case, for Burges
had retired as Under-Secretary of State in the Foreign Office only
a few months previously and in 1795 had received a fine diamond
snuff box, valued at £400, from Catherine II for having 'always been
a good friend of Russia'.[5]

As for the substance of the transaction, Andrew Gale was a plumber
occasionally employed by Smirnov to make small repairs to the house,
which was owned 'by Her Imperial Majesty's Chapel and was occupied by the Embassy Chaplain'. In April 1795 Gale had been engaged
to repair the roof in those places where the lead had burst and leakage
occurred, for which he had tendered an oral estimate of £2. 12s. 6d.
At Christmas time, 'the most usual time with Tradesmen to deliver
Bills', Gale left an account in the amount of £9. 7s. 9d, of which
£8. 1s. 2½d. was for the roof repairs. Some time later a boy called from
Mr Gale demanding payment and was informed by Smirnov through
his servant that the account could not be paid until Gale appeared to
explain the high sum demanded. Some weeks later Gale's brother
appeared to collect the amount due and was similarly apprised. Again
there was no response until one morning Smirnov received a 'printed
Paper, signed by the name of Heighway',[6] indicating that Gale had

---

[3] PRO, FO 65, vol. 33, 10 April 1796.   [4] Ibid.
[5] Burges was a graduate of University College, Oxford. He was called to the bar at
Lincoln's Inn and served as Under-Secretary of State in the Foreign Office from 1789 to
1795.   [6] Richard Heighway practised law at No. 10 Clifford's Inn.

filed suit to collect the debt. 'Concluding from the situation', Smirnov wrote to Vorontsov, 'which I have the honour to fill in this Country, that I could not appear at any Court, without Prejudice to my situation and without derogating from the Privileges attached to it by the Rights [Law] of Nations as belonging to the Mission of Her Imperial Majesty the Empress of all the Russias, I took no further notice of the said Papers'—nor did he of one or two more left at his house subsequently.

On 12 April 1796 Count Vorontsov lodged an official complaint with Lord Grenville (1759–1834), the Secretary of State for Foreign Affairs, appending an English translation of Smirnov's account of what had happened and the court papers.[7] It was, Vorontsov observed to Lord Grenville, the first occasion in his eleven years as minister on which he was obliged to address His Majesty's Government '. . . au sujet d'une infraction aux Droits des gens faite à la mission impériale de Russie par un Tribunal appellé Palace Court de Westminster . . .' and he enclosed 'l'acte autentique fait sur Parcheman qui a servi d'autorisation à ceux qui ont vexé le dit Reverend Smirnove en violation des Droits reconnus par tous les gouvernements et particulièrement par celui de la Grande Bretagne qui est toujours distingué dans leurs observations strictes et inviolables.' Lord Grenville was requested to punish those at fault so that Her Imperial Majesty might be informed of the scrupulous attention being given to maintaining those rights.

Lord Grenville placed the matter in the hands of his under-secretary and close associate, George Hammond (1763–1853),[8] who wrote on 14 April to the Solicitor of the Treasury, Joseph White, instructing White to inquire into the circumstances of the case and report his opinion. In his reply of 19 April 1796, White wrote that Gale, Heighway, and Thompson 'have all been guilty of a breach of the Russian Minister's privileges by suing out an execution against and entering the House of Mr. Smirnove, one of his Domestics. I am therefore of opinion that such Execution is void by Law and if His Excellency hath not pleased to forgive them they by the Attorney General may be prosecuted as the Act of Ann Cap. 12 directs.'[9] All three individuals had been contacted by White and notified that unless they made 'ample atonement to the Russian Minister and obtained his Forgiveness', he would proceed with all legal means to 'bring them to condign punishment for so gross a violation of the Law of Nations'. Heighway and Thompson, he informed Hammond, already were making their apologies but no notice of his letter had been taken by Gale.

[7] Op. cit. (n. 3), 12 April 1796.
[8] Hammond was the first British minister accredited to the United States. He left that post in 1795 to be Under-Secretary of State in the Foreign Office and became close to Lord Grenville.
[9] Op. cit. (n. 3), 19 April 1796.

White proceeded to bring the affair to the attention of the Attorney-General, John Scott (1775–1838), the first Earl of Eldon and later the celebrated Lord Chancellor.[10] While Scott shared the view that the proceedings complained of amounted to a violation of the statute of Queen Anne and a 'breach of the Law of Nations', he took a somewhat different view of the liability of the various persons involved. The plaintiff's attorney, Richard Heighway, was ill in the country when the affidavit was sworn and ignorant of the transaction. Though his name appeared on the writ, it was sued out by his agent, Miles Williamson, who averred complete ignorance of the Revd Smirnov's situation and expressed great contrition. As Heighway had no personal involvement in what had happened he could not be prosecuted under the Act of Anne; and since 'honourable Practice' precluded making use of the affidavit against Williamson, it would be very difficult to prove a case against him. The court officer, Thompson, who sought the writ from Williamson, did know of Smirnov's status but probably acted 'under a persuasion that the Privilege of that Gentleman did not extend to protect his goods from Execution'. His conduct, none the less, Scott described as 'extremely blameable'. Gale, the plaintiff, must have known of Smirnov's situation but probably 'was not aware that that Gentleman's property was protected by the Law of Nations and the Law of the Land'. Both were very contrite. Finally, Scott noted, there was no list of privileged persons in the Palace Court.

An information was being prepared under the Act of Queen Anne, Scott wrote to Lord Grenville on 30 April 1796, and proceedings would go forward unless His Excellency the Ambassador chose to show 'Condescension or Favour' towards them.[11] Ultimately, Vorontsov was merciful, requesting on 4 August 1796, in a letter sent from Richmond to Lord Grenville, that proceedings in the matter be discontinued in view of apologies received.[12]

2

Smirnov's right to claim diplomatic privileges and immunities from civil jurisdiction in this affair was founded on two interrelated principles of international law undergoing crystallization in the eighteenth century. The first was the so-called 'right to chapel' and the second was the extension of diplomatic immunities to members of an ambassador's retinue or suite.

In most European states the religious strife of earlier centuries had abated sufficiently to allow ambassadors, envoys, and residents to

---

[10] In 1801 Lord Eldon supported in the House of Lords the convention with Russia which dissolved the armed neutrality.

[11] Op. cit. (n. 3), 30 April 1796.

[12] PRO, FO 65, vol. 34, 4 August 1796.

exercise freely the religion of their rulers or their state within their own premises.[13] Most publicists treated this right as a natural corollary of the extra-territoriality of embassy property. An ambassador, wrote Wicquefort, 'ought to enjoy in his House so great a Liberty, that no body can there controul his Actions, nor even hinder him from exercising the Religion of his Prince, notwithstanding it be prohibited by the Laws of the Countrey where he is employ'd.'[14] Vattel accepted it as 'certain, that no one can interfere in opposition to the will of a nation, in its religious affairs, without violating its right, and doing it an injury'.[15] It followed, therefore, that the right of an ambassador or lesser diplomatic agent to exercise his religion included the 'right of keeping a chaplain and other subaltern ministers'.[16]

Smirnov's immunity from the civil jurisdiction of English courts derived from his status as a member of the ambassadorial retinue. The ambassador himself was accorded such immunity in order to secure his 'independence', for his security would be 'weakly founded, did not the house in which he lives enjoy an entire exemption, so as to be inaccessible to the ordinary officers of justice'.[17] Ministers, Callières declared, 'are not subject to the Jurisdiction of the Judges of the Country where they have their Residence, and the House ought to be exempted from being searched by Magistrates, and Officers of Justice, being looked upon as the House of the Sovereign whose Ministers they are, and as a sanctuary in that respect.'[18] No juridical action, said Vattel, 'can be directly served on [the publick minister], as he is not subject to the prince or his magistrates.'[19]

Members of the ambassadorial retinue partake of his inviolability and are under his protection because of their connection with and dependence upon him. 'Did not the domesticks and household of a foreign minister solely depend on him', Vattel observed, 'it is known how very easily he might be molested and disturbed in the exercise of his functions.'[20] Many publicists were of the view that 'the retinue of a minister, being exempt from the jurisdiction of the [receiving] state, ought to be subject to the jurisdiction of their master, or of his and their sovereign'.[21]

Whether a chaplain was a *bona fide* member of a diplomatic mission was in England resolved by the simple expedient laid down in the Act

[13] F. de Callières, *The Art of Negotiating with Sovereign Princes* (London, 1716), 96.

[14] A. de Wicquefort, *The Embassador and his Functions* (London, 1716), 266–7.

[15] E. de Vattel, *The Law of Nations, or Principles of the Law of Nature Applied to the Conduct and Affairs of Nations and Sovereigns*, i (London, 1760), 140.

[16] G. F. von Martens, *A Compendium of the Law of Nations Founded on the Treaties and Customs of the Modern Nations of Europe* (London, 1802), 245.

[17] Vattel, *Law of Nations* (n. 15), ii, 165.

[18] Callières, op. cit. (n. 13), 97.

[19] Vattel, *Law of Nations* (n. 15), ii, 163.

[20] Ibid. 167–8.   [21] Martens, op. cit. (n. 16), 237.

of Anne of requiring that every servant of a foreign ambassador be registered in the office of one of the Principal Secretaries of State. Smirnov was duly registered, as he pointed out at once to the officer of the court who sought to serve him with the writ of execution. Even had there been no registration requirement, it seems likely that Smirnov amply fulfilled any *bona fide* criteria. He not only served as chaplain, but also assisted the ambassador in a multitude of tasks, including the ciphering of diplomatic correspondence. Four years after the episode described here he was actually designated chargé d'affaires during the period of Vorontsov's recall from his London post in the last months of Paul I's reign.[22]

3

Smirnov's encounter with the English courts left, so far as the record reveals, no unpleasantness and certainly had no lasting detrimental effects on Anglo-Russian relations. A year later, however, the Foreign Office was again obliged to protect Russian property. In 1797 one William Beaumont, as landlord of a house, No. 8 in Beaumont Street, Marylebone, authorized a broker to distrain the goods of one of his tenants for an arrearage of rent. The broker inadvertently included in his inventory the furniture of another tenant, William Cuthbert, who was a servant of the Russian minister. Vorontsov filed a formal protest, citing the Act of Anne and demanding the prosecution of Beaumont's lawyer ('procureur'), a Mr Alex Trotter.[23] The task of explaining the details of the affair to Lord Grenville was entrusted to Smirnov.

In the event, Trotter promptly instructed his client Beaumont not to disturb the belongings of Cuthbert and so informed the Solicitor of the Treasury, Joseph White, of his actions.[24] Apologies were made to Vorontsov, who expressed his satisfaction, and the issue was carried no further.[25] The law of nations was vindicated, and the principle of the diplomatic immunity of the ambassadorial suite duly re-emphasized.

[22] V. N. Aleksandrenko, *Russkie diplomaticheskie agenty v Londone v XVIII v.* (Warsaw, 1897), i, 545.

[23] PRO, FO 65, vol. 36, 6 March 1797. Mr Trotter kept offices in Great Portland Street.

[24] Ibid.　　　　　　　　　　　　　　　　　　[25] Ibid. 7 March 1797.

Robert Auty's Contribution to Slavonic Studies

By GERALD STONE

THE loss which British Slavonic studies suffered with the death of Robert Auty on 18 August 1978 is nowhere felt more keenly than at Oxford, where he had held the Chair of Comparative Slavonic Philology since 1965. He had been an editor of *Oxford Slavonic Papers* since the inception of the New Series in 1968 and was also a regular contributor, the last occasion being in 1978, the year of his death, when he provided a description of the sixteenth-century Croatian Glagolitic books in the Bodleian Library.[1]

Four years earlier *Oxford Slavonic Papers* published his appreciation of the scholarly achievements of Boris Unbegaun, his predecessor in the Oxford Chair, who had died in 1973.[2] Auty admired Unbegaun's work, and the similarities in the two men's approach to their subject are quite plain. Indeed, it is instructive to re-read Auty's characterization of Unbegaun's attitude to the study of languages, which he describes as being derived 'on the one hand from the philological method which never allows the study of language to move far from the study of actual texts, and on the other hand from the profound conviction that language is primarily to be viewed as an expression and illustration of the life of men'.[3] One cannot help thinking how well these same words might be used to describe Auty's own attitude to his subject. But although the approach of these two scholars was similar or possibly even identical, there is not much overlap in the actual areas of the Slavonic field to which they directed their attention; for whereas Unbegaun's work was concentrated mainly in the Russian field, Auty's centre of gravity was located very firmly in east-central Europe between the Sudetes and Carpathians in the north, and the Adriatic in the south. In some twenty-five articles published in the twenty-five years between 1953 and his death Auty examined various aspects of the evolution of Slavonic literary languages in this area, viz. Czech, Slovak, Slovene, and Serbo-Croat, and these articles taken together must be regarded as the core of his total output (which numbers over 150 items all told) and as his greatest single contribution to Slavonic studies.[4]

[1] 'Sixteenth-century Croatian Glagolitic Books in the Bodleian Library', *Oxford Slavonic Papers*, NS xi (1978), 132–5.

[2] 'B. O. Unbegaun's Contributions to Russian and Slavonic Philology', *Oxford Slavonic Papers*, NS vii (1974), 1–12.   [3] Ibid. 1.

[4] A complete bibliography of Auty's publications accompanies the obituary by Dimitri Obolensky and Anne Pennington in the *Slavonic and East European Review*, lvii (1979), 89–102.

Auty regarded the separate language revivals of the Czechs, Slovaks, Slovenes, Croats, and Serbs as individual but connected aspects of a single movement. In fact, he saw them as part of a phenomenon affecting the whole of Europe, but he believed that its most profound and extensive effects were to be seen in the Slavonic languages and that therefore the evolution of the Slavonic literary languages was a subject which merited special attention. The first fruits of his own work in this field were published in 1953 in an article on the evolution of literary Slovak.[5] Here, in a synthesis of the work done by his predecessors in the field (notably V. Vážný, E. Pauliny, A. Pražák, and P. Király), he showed how the centrifugal tendencies resulting from the decline of Czech as a literary language in the eighteenth century and culminating first in Bernolák's systematic attempt to create a literary language for the Slovaks based on the western dialects were followed by Štúr's successful decision to devise a new form of literary Slovak based on the central dialects but retaining Bernolák's orthography.

A little surprisingly, perhaps, the new type of literary Slovak adopted in 1851 (a modified form of Štúr's language) was quickly accepted by the intelligentsia without controversy and, so far as orthography, phonology, and morphology are concerned, has remained in use since that time without further significant modification. The reasons for its success, including the postulated existence of a kind of spoken κοινή based on the central dialects and used by intellectuals before Štúr appeared on the scene, were examined by Auty in a paper given at the Eighth Congress of the International Federation of Modern Languages and Literatures in 1960.[6]

Auty's interest in the extra-linguistic motivation of linguistic development and, particularly, in the importance of individual codifiers such as Štúr in determining the exact forms adopted in literary languages first came to the fore in an early article dealing with the Czech language revival.[7] Here he asserted that although in the 1780s an atmosphere potentially favourable to a Czech language revival existed in all strata of Bohemian society, it was the influx of Czech-speakers to the towns following the abolition of serfdom which was decisive. Yet the actual form the new language took (according to Auty) was due primarily to the authority of Dobrovský, who envisaged literary Czech as the direct continuation of the language of the sixteenth century, and thereby established the gap between the written and spoken forms of the language which persists to the present day.[8]

[5] 'The Evolution of Literary Slovak', *Transactions of the Philological Society* (1953), 143–60.
[6] 'Dialect, κοινή, and Tradition in the Formation of Literary Slovak', *Slavonic and East European Review*, xxxix (1961), 339–45.
[7] 'Language and Society in the Czech National Revival', *Slavonic and East European Review* xxxv (1956), 241–8.
[8] Ibid. 247–8.

Ideas on the respective roles of individuals and of society at large in the evolution of literary languages were further developed in the paper given by Auty at the Fourth International Congress of Slavists in Moscow in 1958,[9] in which he considered on a comparative basis the extent to which the formation of the Czech and Slovak literary languages and the Croatian literary variant of Serbo-Croat had been directed by Dobrovský, Štúr, and Gaj respectively. He deliberately omitted Slovene from this discussion, because he considered it obvious that no individual, not even Kopitar, had loomed sufficiently large in the history of that language to merit special study,[10] but he did not forsake Slovene altogether and several years later at the Fifth International Congress of Slavists in 1963 he presented a paper surveying the complex historical processes, marked by repeated conflict and compromise, which led to the foundation of literary Slovene.[11] Soon after this he extended his researches beyond the frontiers of the Austrian Empire to the question of Vuk Karadžić's linguistic reforms, thus viewing Serbian developments in the context of the revival movements among the Slavs of Austria.[12] He saw certain parallels in the work of Vuk and Štúr.

The activities of Dobrovský and Jungmann, the two dominant figures in the Czech linguistic and national revival, occupied a leading place in Auty's researches for many years and form the subject of several of his later publications. Particularly memorable is his essay on changing views of the role of Dobrovský in the revival, in which Auty assessed interpretations of the Czech scholar's work by Palacký, Masaryk, V. Brandl, Arne Novák, and also modern Marxist historians, giving most attention to questions of Dobrovský's historicism and patriotism.[13] The separate and distinct tendencies represented by Dobrovský and Jungmann figured prominently in the paper on the formation and development of the Czech literary language which Auty gave at the First International Conference on Soviet and East European Studies held at Banff, Canada, in 1974.[14] He maintained that Dobrovský was primarily a scholar, whereas Jungmann had practical goals in mind,

[9] 'The Linguistic Revival among the Slavs of the Austrian Empire, 1780–1850: the Role of Individuals in the Codification and Acceptance of New Literary Languages', *Modern Language Review*, liii (1958), 392–404.

[10] Ibid. 393.

[11] 'The Formation of the Slovene Literary Language against the Background of the Slavonic National Revival', *Slavonic and East European Review*, xli (1963), 391–402.

[12] 'Вукова језичка реформа у свјетлу језичког препорода међу Славенима аустријске монархије', *Београдски универзитет. Анали Филолошког факултета*, v (1965) (Belgrade, 1966), 9–14.

[13] 'Changing Views on the Role of Dobrovský in the Czech National Revival', in: *The Czech Renascence of the Nineteenth Century*, ed. P. Brock and H. Gordon Skilling (1970), 14–25.

[14] 'Problems of the Formation and Development of the Czech Literary Language', in: T. F. Magner (ed.), *Slavic Linguistics and Language Teaching* (Cambridge, Mass., 1976), 82–8.

but that they were in full agreement in their basic conception of the literary language.[15]

Some of the other subjects, within the general framework of the development of the Slavonic literary languages, to which Auty contributed are: the indeclinable nouns in Czech,[16] orthographic innovations and controversies,[17] the role of purism,[18] methods of lexical enrichment,[19] and the language of medieval and early modern Slavonic literatures.[20] We should also not forget his work on Ignjat Alojzije Brlić, author of the *Grammatik der illyrischen Sprache* (1833), in the course of which he made use of the Brlić family archive.[21]

Although Auty's main interest was in tracing the development of the Slavonic literary languages, the study of Old Church Slavonic occupies a position only slightly less prominent among his scholarly activities. Apart from the well-known *Handbook of Old Church Slavonic*, produced in collaboration with Grigore Nandriş,[22] he wrote a number of articles on this subject, covering such topics as the sources of the Glagolitic alphabet[23] and the interpretation of passages in the *Vita Constantini*.[24] Three of his Old Church Slavonic articles deal with problems of Latin and German borrowings,[25] including the word *oplatŭ* 'the host, bread of the communion service', recorded in the Kiev Missal. It had been supposed that the source of this word was either Latin *oblata, oblatum* or Upper German **oplāte* (reconstructed from Middle High German

[15] Ibid. 84. See also R. Auty, 'Jazykové koncepce u Dobrovského a Jungmanna', in: A. Jedlička *et al.* (eds.), *Slovanské spisovné jazyky v době obrození* (Prague, 1974), 122–4.

[16] 'A Note on the Indeclinable Nouns of Modern Czech', in: R. Magidoff *et al.* (eds.), *Studies in Slavic Linguistics and Poetics in Honor of Boris O. Unbegaun* (New York–London, 1968), 11–14.

[17] 'Orthographical Innovations and Controversies among the Western and Southern Slavs during the Slavonic National Revival', *Slavonic and East European Review*, xlvi (1968), 324–32.

[18] 'The Role of Purism in the Development of the Slavonic Literary Languages', *Slavonic and East European Review*, li (1973), 335–43.

[19] 'Sources and Methods of Lexical Enrichment in the Slavonic Language-revivals of the Early Nineteenth Century', *The Slavic Word. Proceedings of the International Slavistic Colloquium at UCLA. September 11–16, 1970*, ed. D. S. Worth (The Hague–Paris, 1972), 41–56.

[20] 'Literary Language and Literary Dialect in Medieval and Early Modern Slavonic Literatures', *Slavonic and East European Review*, lvi (1978), 192–201.

[21] 'The Linguistic Work of Ignjat Alojzije Brlić (1795–1855)', *Filologija*, 3 (Zagreb, 1962), 5–22.

[22] R. Auty, *Handbook of Old Church Slavonic*, pt. 2, *Texts and Glossary* (1960). (Pt. 1, *Old Church Slavonic Grammar* is by Nandriş.)

[23] 'Old and New Ideas on the Sources of the Glagolitic Alphabet', in: *Константин-Кирил философ. Доклади от симпозиума, посветен на 1100-годишнината от смъртта му* (Sofia, 1971), 41–4.

[24] 'The Gospel and Psalter of Cherson: Syriac or Russian?', in: *To Honor Roman Jakobson* (The Hague–Paris, 1967), 114–17; 'Slavonic Letters before St. Cyril: the Evidence of the *Vita Constantini*', in: *Studia palaeoslovenica*, ed. B. Havránek (Prague, 1971), 27–30.

[25] 'Old Church Slavonic *oplatŭ*', *Revue des études slaves*, xl (1964) (Mélanges André Vaillant), 13–15; 'The Western Lexical Elements in the Kiev Missal', in: W. Kraus *et al.* (eds.), *Slawisch-deutsche Wechselbeziehungen in Sprache, Literatur und Kultur* (Berlin, 1969), 3–6; 'Lateinisches und Althochdeutsches im Kirchenslavischen Wortschatz', *Slovo. Časopis Staroslavenskog instituta*, xxv/xxvi (Zagreb, 1976), 169–74.

oblâte), but it was difficult to see why it should appear in Old Church Slavonic as a masculine *o*-stem. Auty solved this problem by providing a more plausible source, viz. Old High German *oplāt/*oblāt (reconstructed from the recorded apocopated Middle High German form *oblât*).[26] He was of the opinion that all the western loanwords in the Kiev Missal were of Old High German origin, with the single exception of *prěfacija*.[27] His German linguistic expertise aided his discernment in such matters.

There appear to have been several factors in Auty's move from German to Slavonic studies. One of them was a visit to Prague in 1937 (at which time he had just been appointed assistant lecturer in German at Cambridge). Another was the influence of his Cambridge colleague N. B. Jopson, whose courses in Old Church Slavonic he attended in 1938–9.[28] Owing to his early connection with Prague and also to the central position occupied by Czech in his academic interests, it is believed by some that Czech was the first Slavonic language to draw his interest. In fact, however, it was Russian which first attracted him, and this, as he once told me, was a result of reading Maurice Baring's novel *Tinker's Leave*, which is set in Russia.

Nevertheless, there are few Russian items in Auty's bibliography. Although he had a good knowledge of Russian, and was particularly well-informed on Russian historical grammar (a subject on which he regularly lectured to undergraduates with supreme competence), he did comparatively little research in the Russian field. There are, however, two Russian items of importance. The first is a paper read to the Philological Society in 1974 on the problem of *akan'e*.[29] Though making no new attempt to solve the problem, it is a highly efficient survey of existing suggestions as to how, when, and why Russian acquired this feature. The second important Russian item is the *Companion to Russian Studies*, edited by Auty and Dimitri Obolensky,[30] the second volume of which contains Auty's useful summary of the history of the Russian language and his brief account of early types of writing in Russia.[31]

Though not primarily concerned with the interpretation of imaginative literature, Auty did have peripheral interests in this area, and they led to the production of a few articles on literary themes, including one

[26] 'Old Church Slavonic *oplatŭ*' (n. 25).

[27] 'Western Lexical Elements' (n. 25), 6.

[28] See R. Auty, 'Norman Brooke Jopson (1890–1969)', *Slavonic and East European Review*, xlvii (1969), 304.

[29] 'The Problem of Russian *akan'je*', *Transactions of the Philological Society 1974* (Oxford, 1975), 146–58.

[30] *Companion to Russian Studies*: i. *An Introduction to Russian History* (Cambridge, 1976), and ii. *An Introduction to Russian Language and Literature* (Cambridge, 1977).

[31] 'The Russian Language', ibid. ii, 1–40, and 'Russian Writing and Printing. A: Writing', ibid. ii, 41–7.

on the poems written in German by the Slovene poet Francè Prešeren.[32] Probably of greater importance, however, are his three publications on the Czech medieval love-lyric. The texts of three dawn-songs, with English translations and commentary by Auty, were included in a symposium published in 1965,[33] and to one of them (described by him as 'an inconsistent but intriguing mixture of courtly and popular elements')[34] he devoted a special study which appeared the following year.[35] But his last, and best, piece of work on the Czech medieval love-lyric, published in the first volume of the New Series of *Oxford Slavonic Papers*, surveyed the entire genre.[36] He was of course particularly well equipped for research in this field owing to his profound knowledge not only of Czech but also of German medieval literature.

In order to view Auty's scholarly achievement in context it is worth recalling his links with Prague and his regard for the ideas of the Prague Linguistic Circle, several of whose members were his friends. One question which was present or implicit in many of his deliberations, viz. that of man's ability, either collectively or individually, to influence the course of language development, was simultaneously coming to the fore as a general sociolinguistic problem. According to Haugen the term 'language planning' was first used when Uriel Weinreich gave it as the title of a seminar held at Columbia University in 1957.[37] Auty, however, was evidently not attracted by this current, aspiring rather to follow the lines indicated in the work of the Prague Circle, particularly that of Havránek. Auty's writings, unlike those of Unbegaun, are rarely provocative or controversial, and it would be unreasonable to maintain that they are always distinguished by great originality. But they are undoubtedly imbued with the broadmindedness and clarity which were characteristic of his method.

[32] 'Prešeren's German poems', *Oxford Slavonic Papers*, NS vi (1973), 1–11.
[33] A. T. Hatto, *Eos* (The Hague, 1965), 579–87.
[34] R. Auty, 'The Medieval Czech Love-lyric', *Oxford Slavonic Papers*, NS i (1968), 19.
[35] 'Zum alttschechischen Tagelied Přěčekaje vše zlě strážě', in: D. Gerhardt et al. (eds.), *Orbis Scriptus: Dmitrij Tschiževskij zum 70. Geburtstag* (Munich, 1966), 75–9.
[36] 'Medieval Czech Love-lyric' (n. 34).
[37] E. Haugen, *Language Conflict and Language Planning. The Case of Modern Norwegian* (Cambridge, Mass., 1966), 355, n. 3.

Language and Nationality in East-Central Europe 1750–1950

By ROBERT AUTY

This paper is a slightly shortened and edited version of the four De Carle lectures which Robert Auty delivered in July 1975 at Otago University, New Zealand. The editors have provided the footnotes.

I. LANGUAGES AND NATIONS

THE territories lying between Germany and Russia, and bounded on the north by the Baltic and on the south by the Aegean and Adriatic seas, present to the linguist, ethnographer, or historian a pattern of the utmost complexity. As a result of the final surge of the early medieval migration of peoples, and of a thousand years of later conquests, colonization, and national struggles the variety of national groups and speech-communities in this region is unsurpassed in the rest of Europe. At least fifteen clearly recognizable languages are spoken in it, to say nothing of the sometimes extreme dialectal variety within those languages. Today most of these languages are in use in the countries of the region as fully fledged literary languages, standardized in form and usage, and employed for all the social, administrative, and aesthetic purposes of the modern world. This situation, however, is of relatively recent origin.

In 1750 the only languages of this region which were used without functional restriction, at all levels and for all purposes, were Swedish (in Finland), German (in the Baltic Provinces and the Habsburg domains), Polish (in the Polish Commonwealth), Greek, and Turkish (both in the Turkish Empire). To these might be added languages with accepted status: Latin, the official language of Hungary and Poland and the universal language of scholarship and higher education; Russian, used marginally in the Baltic Provinces; and, more important, Italian in Dalmatia and Dubrovnik. Of the other languages of the region Hungarian enjoyed literary cultivation, but was inadequate for more varied social functions; Czech was remembered as a once widely used medium of literature, scholarship, and administration, but had now been almost completely degraded to the status of a peasant patois or (among the lower urban classes) a corrupt Germanized jargon. The most important local varieties of Serbo-Croat were the so-called *Slavenosrpski* of the Vojvodina, an unstable amalgam of vernacular Serbian, Church Slavonic, and Russian; the kajkavic literary dialect of Zagreb whose currency hardly extended beyond the confines of Civil Croatia; the Slavonian literary dialect which developed in the eighteenth century and was equally limited in territorial scope and influence; and, finally, the declining literary language of Dubrovnik.

In surveying this picture it is important to bear in mind that at this time (at least in the region with which I am concerned) language was viewed functionally. In the many bilingual or multilingual areas different languages would be used for particular purposes. In Upper Hungary, for example, a man might use Slovak at home, German for commercial transactions in town, Hungarian with officials or social superiors, Latin in school or on certain official occasions; similarly, in the central Balkans a man would easily move, for example, between Macedonian Slavonic, Greek, and Turkish with similar functional specialization. National consciousness, so far as it existed, did not bear its modern character; and the deliberate cultivation of a vernacular as an expression of national identity or national pride was not yet found.

If we briefly survey the situation a hundred years later we find that it has changed dramatically. In Finland an intensive scholarly interest in the national language and traditions soon gave rise to a new national literature. Björn Collinder has shown the 1850s to be the period of the breakthrough of the Finnish language.[1] In Estonia, too, from the 1820s a generation of Estonian intellectuals reacted against the unquestioning acceptance of German literature and civilization and began to discuss the active cultivation of the Estonian language and to create a secular Estonian literature. The first great triumph of this literature was the national epic *Kalevipoeg* (composed by F. R. Kreutzwald on the basis of popular poetry), which began to appear in 1857 in Dorpat. A similar process was under way among the Latvians, who also began to cultivate the vernacular in didactic and scholarly works, in journals, and in secular poetry and prose. Here, too, by the 1860s it was possible to speak of a new national literature. The development of the Lithuanian literary language was slower, despite the inauguration of Lithuanian secular poetry in Prussia in the 1770s by K. Donelaitis. Nevertheless, by the second half of the nineteenth century the beginnings of a new Lithuanian literary language were emerging, notwithstanding the pressure of Russianization.

The partitions of Poland, far from handicapping the development of the national language there, positively stimulated a revived poetical literature of real genius in the 1830s and 1840s. Although political oppression or restrictions limited its use in administration and public life, Polish never ceased to be a great language of civilization.

In the Habsburg domains stirrings of national consciousness had been increasingly felt throughout the eighteenth century and were powerfully stimulated by local reactions to the measures of administrative

[1] B. Collinder, *Comparative Grammar of the Uralic Languages* (Uppsala, 1960), 16.

centralization introduced by Maria Theresa and Joseph II, and especially by the latter's endeavour, prompted by purely rationalistic motives, to introduce German as the universal language of administration. Among the Czechs antiquarian interest in the past history and civilization of Bohemia led to an intensive preoccupation with the vernacular which, from the 1820s, developed into a nationalist movement no longer limited to linguistic and literary aims. By 1850 the new national literature was flourishing and the social prestige and currency of the Czech language was rapidly increasing. The revival of the Slovene literary language also dates from the latter part of the eighteenth century and shows a similar movement from merely scholarly endeavours to the creation of a new literature and the further extension of the vernacular to other social spheres. Here, too, the new linguistic situation was clearly outlined by the 1850s.

The Hungarian 'language renewal' (*nyelvújítás*) which began in the 1770s was more radical in its effects than any of the contemporary processes among the other peoples of the region. By the 1850s the language was thoroughly modernized, well-nigh completely purged of obvious foreign elements, and enriched by the writings of a series of poets of the highest talent. Moreover, the upsurge of Hungarian national feeling had called forth a reaction in some of the other peoples of Hungary. It is partly a reaction of this kind that gave rise to the concept of a separate Slovak language: and this also, after certain vicissitudes, occupied a secure position among the literary languages of Central Europe by the middle of the 1850s. Moreover, Hungarian demands for the Hungarian language to have official status throughout the territories of the Holy Crown, including Croatia, played no small part in stimulating the movement among the Croats which culminated in the establishment of a unified and accepted form of their language. This movement ran parallel with similar activities among the Serbs of the Vojvodina, with the result that a common Serbo-Croatian literary language was for the first time officially recognized to exist in the Vienna Agreement of 1850, signed by a number of Serbian and Croatian scholars and writers. Finally, the national movement among the Rumanians of Transylvania in the last decades of the eighteenth century, which exercised a profound influence on the revival and later development of the Rumanian literary language, must be regarded, at least in part, as a similar reaction to Hungarian pretensions.

In the Balkans the establishment of the independent Greek kingdom in 1830 compelled the appearance of the language question in a new form. The classicizing *katharévousa* was in the ascendant in the mid-century but was soon to be challenged by the revival of demotic. Of the other Balkan vernaculars Bulgarian was already establishing itself as a language of literature and education, firmly based on popular dialects, though it was not until the latter part of the century that it achieved stability. The development of the Albanian literary vernacular lagged behind that of its neighbours; but here too the Albanian scholar A. Kostallari notes that a new period in the history of the literary language began with the appearance of the *Ëvetari shqip* (Albanian ABC) of Naum Bredhi-Veqilharxhi in 1845, and also that in the 1860s we see the first deliberate tendencies towards a rapprochement between the two variant literary dialects of Albanian.[2]

Of the literary languages current in the Balkans today Macedonian had not yet made an appearance in the 1850s, though elements of the Slavonic dialects of Macedonia can be detected in certain works. The development of a deliberate Macedonian linguistic separatism is a later phenomenon, belonging for the most part to the twentieth century, and it was not until the 1940s that Macedonian fully achieved the status of a literary language.

II. LINGUISTIC REVOLUTION: PATTERNS OF CHANGE

Thus in a century or less the number of the languages in our region which were deemed suitable for use in literature or in cultivated society had more than doubled. Not all of them were in official use, but all were being consciously developed with the aim of becoming functionally equivalent to the traditionally dominant, accepted languages. By the mid-twentieth century, after a further century of linguistic evolution, every one of the languages I have mentioned had official status, all were media in which literary works of quality and often of genius had been written, and almost all were fully stabilized and codified. While the history of each language has its specific features, the individual processes are all exponents of a general movement, the common features of which I should like to explore and characterize below.

Fundamental to this movement is a change in the attitude to language. Until the eighteenth century language in East-Central Europe was a functional tool, useful or necessary for specific forms of social activity. The practice of literature was, it is true, one such form of activity, but this was exclusively reserved to those languages which were hallowed by tradition (primarily Latin and Greek) or which had achieved respectability through a long apprenticeship in medieval or early modern times. Of the indigenous languages of the region (if we set aside German) only Polish, Czech, Hungarian, and certain forms of Serbo-Croat (notably the literary dialect of Dubrovnik) had been fully accepted as literary languages; but literary Czech had fallen into disuse and had lost its social prestige, while the other languages

[2] A. Kostallari, *Gjuha e Sotme letrare Shqipe dhe disa Probleme Themelore te Drejtshkrimit te Saj* (Tirana, 1973), 108–10.

mentioned were all to a greater or lesser extent in decline, hard pressed or even dominated by Latin or by western languages with greater authority and prestige.

In the latter part of the eighteenth century a new attitude to language began to take shape. Each language came to be thought of as the unique and characteristic expression of the nation that spoke it, possessing equal rights with any other language. The first signs of a new interest in vernacular languages manifested itself in the work of scholars and teachers. Sooner or later, in all the territories concerned, this theoretical interest became transformed into an active cultivation of the given language; and this in its turn frequently merged with political movements which claimed equality of rights for the nations of whom the languages were the foremost symbol and expression.

We may accordingly distinguish three periods in the East-Central European linguistic revolution: the scholarly and didactic phase, which corresponds with the late Enlightenment; the period of romantic nationalism before it took on an overtly political character; and the period of consolidation and normalization of the new literary languages. These periods are not coterminous in all the territories, but the general characteristics of the process are everywhere comparable. We shall consider how these three phases found expression in the different territories.

In the first decades of the eighteenth century central and northern Europe entered on a period of relatively peaceful development after the destructive and debilitating wars of the previous century. The Turkish threat which had struck at the very heart of Europe was finally lifted after the successful defence of Vienna in 1683 and the liberation of Hungary and Slavonia, which was confirmed by the peace of Karlowitz (Karlovci) in 1699. Peace was, however, not fully restored to Hungary until 1711, when the peace of Szatmár marked the end of the civil war in which Ferenc Rákóczi II and his *kuruc* rebels had unsuccessfully pitted themselves against the forces of the Emperor. Similarly, in the north the peace of Nystad (Uusikaupunki) marked the end of the long drawn out Northern War; and, while the elimination of Swedish influence in the Baltic Provinces was probably a negative factor in the cultural progress of that region, the stability of the new regime was more conducive to intellectual development than the chaotic conditions of war.

In these circumstances new intellectual currents from western Europe, especially from France, began gradually to penetrate into East-Central Europe, sometimes indirectly, through German mediation, but often also through the study of the original works of western thinkers and writers. In two spheres in particular the thought and intellectual practices of the Enlightenment made themselves felt in our region from the mid-eighteenth century onwards: in historical study and in the reform of education. Developments in both these spheres had great importance for the history of the national languages.

(a) Czech

Historical research based on the critical study of documents had begun to develop into an exact discipline in seventeenth-century France. The influence of this new science is particularly to be observed in Bohemia. The efforts of the Empress Maria Theresa and her son Joseph II to modernize and centralize the administration of their far-flung domains gave rise to feelings of local particularism in those provinces which felt their interests affected by the new measures— above all Hungary and Bohemia. One expression of this *Landespatriotismus* was a heightened interest in national traditions and origins. In Bohemia especially the nobility, who were the class most nearly affected by the centralizing policies, supported the research of scholars into the antiquities and historical records of their country. The former uncritical repetition of traditional legends and superstitions was replaced by a number of historical studies of real critical quality. Foremost among these was the critical edition, made by Gelasius Dobner, of a Latin translation of the sixteenth-century Czech chronicle of Václav Hájek.[3] In his detailed commentary on this work, which had been regarded as an authoritative source for the history of Bohemia, Dobner was able to show, from his critical study of documents, that much of it was not history but legend. By clearing away uncritical beliefs and prejudices Dobner laid the foundations of modern Czech historiography, and at the same time stimulated interest in the genuine documents of the past. The work of Dobner and other scholars working on similar lines was supported by members of the Bohemian nobility through encouragement and financial patronage. Scholarly interest in the Czech national past was also fostered by learned societies, first by the short-lived *Societas incognitorum* of Olomouc in Moravia (1746–52), and then, more lastingly, by the 'Private Scientific Society' ('Privatgesellschaft der Wissenschaften'), later to be known as the 'Bohemian [from 1790 'Royal Bohemian'] Scientific Society' ('[Königliche] Böhmische Gesellschaft der Wissenschaften'), which was founded in about 1770. The proceedings of this society included several articles on the literary and linguistic history of Bohemia. The importance of the nobility in the development of Czech national feeling at this time is illustrated by the fact that the chief begetter of the Scientific Society was a nobleman, Ignaz Edler von Born, and that one of his chief collaborators was Count

---

[3] G. Dobner (ed.), *Annales Bohemorum e Bohemia editione Latine redditi et notis illustrati, a P. Victorino a S. Cruce e Scholiis Piis*, i–vi (Prague, 1761).

F. J. Kinský, himself the author of an important 'defence' of the Czech language, which appeared anonymously in 1773.[4] A prominent member of the Society was Josef Dobrovský, who was to become the chief codifier of the Czech literary language and the founder of comparative Slavonic philology. Destined to be a Jesuit (until the dissolution of the Order in 1773), Dobrovský devoted himself first to Biblical studies. These led him to the study of Old Church Slavonic, and this in turn stimulated his interest in the other Slavonic languages, above all Czech, which he had only learned to speak in his schooldays at Německý Brod (now Havlíčkův Brod). The principal fruit of Dobrovský's study of his own language was his grammar.[5] This was the most scholarly and systematic description of the Czech language that had ever appeared. It was in essence a codification of the literary language in use in Bohemia at the time of the eclipse of the Bohemian state after the Battle of the White Mountain in 1621. Dobrovský was not aiming at a revival of this language. He did not believe that it would ever again attain the position in the national life that it had occupied in the late sixteenth century, but he wished to encourage the knowledge, among cultivated men, of the finest monuments of what he regarded as the 'golden age' of Czech literature.

Thus, in Bohemia, the combination of the critical scholarly methods characteristic of the Enlightenment and a preoccupation with national identity, which resulted in part from the reaction to Habsburg centralism, led to the linguistic work of Dobrovský, the significance of which was far greater than he himself imagined.

After the turn of the century, and in particular after 1815, a new generation of Czech intellectuals turned their attention to the language. It was now no longer a question of scholarly research alone, but of activity directed towards restoring the language to its earlier status. The leader of these endeavours, Josef Jungmann (1773–1847), only 14 years younger than Dobrovský, while criticizing the coldly dispassionate attitude of the older scholar to his subject, nevertheless based his work on Dobrovský's codification of the language. The language described by Dobrovský, if viewed from the standpoint of a twentieth-century linguist, might be thought to have two defects. It represented essentially the language of the late sixteenth century, and thus differed in many respects from the spoken vernacular of 1800; and it was firmly based on the Czech of Bohemia and was thus somewhat removed from the dialects of Moravia, and still more from those of the Slovaks, who were still regarded by many as sharing a common literary language with the

---

[4] *Erinnerung über einen wichtigen Gegenstand, von einem Böhmen* (Prague, 1773).

[5] J. Dobrovský, *Ausführliches Lehrgebäude der böhmischen Sprache zur gründlichen Erlernung derselben für Deutsche, zur vollkommenern Kenntniß für Böhmen* (Prague, 1809). Second edition: *Lehrgebäude der böhmischen Sprache. Zum Theile verkürzt, zum Theile umgearbeitet und vermehrt* (Prague, 1819). Both editions reprinted Prague, 1940.

Czechs. But theoretical objections of this kind, though they were some-times raised, had next to no effect on the development of the language. Dobrovský's codification, made for purposes of scholarship, became a weapon of national self-assertion. The work of Jungmann and his associates consisted in the extension and modernization of the vocabu-lary and in the encouragement of the use of the language. In this they were completely successful. By the middle of the century Czech was fully re-established as a multi-functional literary language.

(b) Hungarian

In Hungary, too, the eighteenth century saw a heightening of national consciousness and the influence of rationalistic scholarship. Interest in the national past inspired a number of historical works in Transylvania in the late seventeenth and early eighteenth centuries. This interest derived from local circumstances: Transylvania had been the most independent of the Hungarian territories, holding off the Turkish assaults and then becoming the base of the *kuruc* revolt against the Habsburgs.

In Hungary, as in Bohemia, awareness of the national past and solicitude for the national identity soon brought with it a preoccupation with linguistic questions. In Hungary, however, in contrast to Bohemia, it cannot be said that the period of objective study and codification of the language preceded the active, conscious movement for its reform and modernization. The pressure of German was clearly felt in the 1770s and a number of writers began to assert the role of Hungarian in the national life and to take steps to equip their language with all the resources needed for the creation of a modern literature and for the employment of the vernacular in all spheres of modern life. Professor Aurélien Sauvageot has graphically characterized the situation of the Hungarian language in about 1770. 'Le choix qui se posait de la manière la plus pressante à l'élite hongroise vers les années 1770 était assez simple: ou s'exprimer désormais en allemand ou faire du hongrois une langue susceptible de rivaliser soit avec l'allemand, qui se trouvait lui-même en pleine rénovation, soit avec le français dont le prestige était inégalé.'[6] Already in the 1770s a number of young writers began to translate and imitate French literary works and in the process to forge new words and expressions. 'Only in our own language', wrote one of these authors, György Bessenyei, 'can we successfully educate the people.'[7] Other writers (Dávid Baróti Szabó, András Dugonics) took their inspiration more from classical (especially Latin) literature, but also found it necessary to create a whole new vocabulary in order adequately to emulate their classical models.

[6] A. Sauvageot, *L'Édification de la langue hongroise* (Paris, 1971), 228.
[7] V. Tolnai, *A nyelvújítás elmélete és története* (Budapest, 1929), 44.

E

Side by side with this practical activity in the field of language renewal the scholarly study of the Hungarian language was proceeding apace. Two pioneers of historical-comparative linguistics, J. Sajnovics and S. Gyarmathi, established the existence of the Finno-Ugrian language-family.[8] Thus the foundations of Finno-Ugrian comparative philology were laid at a time when the affinities between the Indo-European languages, though recognized, had not yet been scientifically analysed. The two Hungarian linguists nevertheless received scant gratitude from their compatriots, who set little store by kinship with the distant Finns and the obscure Lapps. The process of enrichment of the language was given a powerful impetus by the appearance of the first Hungarian newspaper *A Magyar Hírmondó* in 1780. The need to comment on current affairs and on varied intellectual concerns further encouraged the creation and use of new words. The first editor of this journal set his face against foreign words, against the contamination and corruption of Hungarian by foreign elements.

Thus, in the last quarter of the eighteenth century the reform of the Hungarian language was in full swing, characterized by two tendencies: towards the enrichment and modernization of the language so that it might vie in all fields with the great languages of the West; and towards the intensification of its national character, by the exclusion of foreign elements. For some scholars and writers, however, the movement of reform was too rapid; and objection was expressed especially to the excessive creation of new words. Usage and tradition should govern the literary language, it was argued. This conservative point of view found expression especially in the so-called *Debrecen Grammar*.[9] The principle of this work was that the language should be regarded as static, and should be preserved and cultivated in the form in which it had come to exist. The introduction of new words was not excluded, but such words should conform to rules of word-formation already existing in the language. There is a certain similarity between the Debrecen grammar and the grammar of Dobrovský in that both attempt to codify an existing literary language. But the scholars of Debrecen consciously regarded their grammar as a prescriptive work for writers to follow, while Dobrovský expressed no opinions of this kind, contenting himself with the scholarly exercise of codification without specifying the uses to which his work might be put.

Thus, there crystallized in late eighteenth-century Hungary the opposed groups of *Neologists* (*neológusok*) and *Orthologists* (*ortológusok*). That the former group ultimately routed their opponents was in great

---

[8] J. Sajnovics, *Demonstratio idioma Ungarorum et Lapponum idem esse* (Nagyszombat/Trnava, 1770); S. Gyarmathi, *Affinitas linguae hungaricae cum linguis fennicae originis grammatice demonstrata* (Göttingen, 1799).

[9] *Magyar Grammatika, mellyet készített Debreczenbenn egy magyar társaság* (Debrecen, 1795).

part due to the shrewd and tenacious activity of Ferenc Kazinczy (1759–1831). From 1801 to 1819 Kazinczy propagated the neologist view against the orthologists. The struggle was a bitter one, but by the time Kazinczy formulated his views on the language question in the journal *Tudományos Gyűjtemény* in 1819 the neologist cause was victorious. Kazinczy considered it right and proper for individuals, and through them the community, to try to improve their language, not merely by increasing its functional possibilities and by intensifying its national character, but by making it aesthetically more attractive. The aims of Kazinczy and of the movement to which he gave form and direction have been aptly summarized by V. Tolnai, the historian of the Hungarian language renewal, as the enrichment, the purification, and the embellishment of the language (*nyelvbővítés, nyelvtisztítás, nyelvszépítés*).[10] The pursuit of these aims involved the rejection of reliance on natural development and educated usage. It demanded the deliberate and systematic intervention by individuals in the linguistic process. Kazinczy was thus a pioneer of what has come to be known as language-planning.

The movement of language reform thus progressed more rapidly in Hungary than in Bohemia. In the latter country a period of growing national awareness, expressed largely in scholarly terms, was followed by the more practical efforts to revive and modernize the language; in Hungary scholarly codification and active language reform proceeded side by side from the beginning. The explanation lies no doubt in the higher degree of national consciousness in Hungary in the early eighteenth century. The semi-independent development of Transylvania and the *kuruc* rebellion of the early eighteenth century brought the national issue to the surface at a time when in Bohemia it was still dormant. In Bohemia it was not until the reforms of Maria Theresa and Joseph II that deliberate attention began to be paid to the question of national identity; and it took some time before such preoccupations took shape in a campaign to restore and extend the use of the Czech language. No doubt we must also bear in mind the fact that in the eighteenth century the Hungarian literary language, though functionally restricted, was nevertheless in a more flourishing state than its Czech counterpart. Hungarian required renewal, Czech revival.

(c) Slovak

The growth of Hungarian national feeling in the eighteenth century soon stimulated reactions among the non-Hungarian populations which inhabited the Hungarian kingdom proper, as well as Croatia and Transylvania, either in compact groups or, especially in the towns, intermingled with Hungarians. In the northern and north-western counties the mass of the population spoke Slavonic dialects which,

[10] Tolnai, op. cit. (n. 7).

while varying amongst themselves, nevertheless shared many common features and were closely related to the Czech dialects of Moravia and Bohemia. These dialects had never formed the basis of a written language. When the need had arisen for the speakers of them to write in the vernacular, as against the official Latin or the *lingue franche*, Hungarian and German, Czech had been used. In the course of the seventeenth and eighteenth centuries many local elements had found their way into these Czech texts without, however, giving rise to anything like a specific or uniform literary language. These Slavs of Upper Hungary were known to the Hungarians as *tót*, a word sometimes used for Slavs of other parts of the kingdom. In their own language, as well as in Czech, they were generally known as *Slováci, slovenský*, words which similarly meant simply 'Slav' without further definition. These are the people whom we know today as the Slovaks, the general appellation having taken on a specific meaning since they developed feelings of national identity. We can witness this process of developing self-awareness among the Slovaks in the early eighteenth century. It is illustrated by a controversy which arose in the 1720s. A Hungarian lawyer, Mihály Bencsik of Nagyszombat/Trnava, presented to the Hungarian Diet which assembled in Pozsony/Pressburg in 1722 a series of propositions summarizing the public law of the Hungarian kingdom. In one of these he repeated an old legend to the effect that, when the Hungarians had irrupted into the Danube valley in the ninth century, the Slavs then resident there under the rule of their monarch Svätopluk had sold to the invaders their whole land 'Terram, Aquam et Gramen' for the price of a white horse, saddled and bridled, and had thereby become for all time subject to the Hungarians as 'colonists' and 'guests'. Six years later a Slovak priest, J. B. Magin, published an 'Apologia for the County of Trenčín', in which he rejected Bencsik's thesis and strongly argued that the Slovaks were in no way subject to the Hungarians but that they, like the Hungarians, were free members of the *natio hungarica* with equal rights. Moreover, as Slavs, they belong to a race which is ancient and famous and inhabits large areas of the earth. While the level of scholarship of Magin's riposte is not much higher than that of Bencsik's work, the attitude reflects the new interest in the national past stimulated by the Hungarian pretensions, as well as the first stirrings of Slovak national feeling. Such tendencies found increasingly frequent expression as the century proceeded. They are particularly characteristic of the period after 1780. The concept of a Slovak nationality is clearly expressed by Juraj Papánek in his work *De regno, regibusque Slavorum*.[11] It is interesting that he deals with the question of the absence of a national appellation.

[11] J. Papánek, *De regno, regibusque Slavorum atque cum prisci civilis, et ecclesiastici, tum hujus aevi statu gentis Slavae* . . . (Quinque-Ecclesiis, 1780).

It may well be asked, he says, why the Slavs of Hungary have no specific territorial name, like the Moravians, Russians, or other related peoples. Why are they not named, for example, after the river Hron or Váh? The answer is simple: they are called *Slováк* because they have retained the original Slavonic language uncorrupted and therefore, by implication, are entitled to the name Slav without further modification. In other works this conception is elaborated further. It was, moreover, in the Moravian empire that Saints Cyril and Methodius, the Apostles of the Slavs, had exercised their mission in the ninth century, so that in religion too the Slovaks have primacy over other Slavonic nations. In this way scholarship created a theoretical basis for a Slovak nationality before an accepted Slovak literary language had been established.

A first attempt in this direction was made in the late 1780s by Anton Bernolák, a native of Orava in north-west Slovakia who had studied in Trnava/Nagyszombat, in Vienna, and at the General Seminary of Bratislava/Pressburg. It seems that his intention to codify the Slovak language on the basis mainly of western dialects dates from his time at the General Seminary. This was one of a number of such institutions founded by Joseph II in different provinces of the Empire in order to train priests in accordance with his own principles of liberal and practically oriented Catholicism. One of the features of the training was that the student-priests were encouraged to use the vernacular languages. In 1787 Bernolák published a short treatise on orthography in which he proposed a spelling system appropriate for his native tongue. He wished moreover to purify it of the 'errors' introduced from Czech: '. . . ad orthographiam, et pronunciationem pannonio-slavam excolendam, et ab erroribus, ex pronunciatione, et orthographia bohemica in nostram linguam derivatis, repurgandam . . .'.[12] This was followed in 1790 by a full-scale grammar of Slovak, the first of its kind ever to be published.[13] Based largely on western dialects, this language enjoyed a considerable vogue among the Slovak Catholic intelligentsia for about forty years. Even though the language codified by Bernolák was not destined to become the finally accepted literary language of the Slovaks, it proved its viability in practice; and thus in this instance the culmination of the movement of Enlightenment scholarship among the Slovak intelligentsia coincided with the dissemination of the newly codified language for practical purposes.

[12] A. Bernolák, *Dissertatio philologico-critica de literis Slavorum, de divisione illarum nec non accentibus. Cum adnexa linguae Slavonicae per regnum Hungariae usitatae compendiosa simul, et facili orthographia, ad systema scholarum nationalium in ditionibus caesareo-regiis introductum plene accommodata* (Posonii/Bratislava, 1787). Reprinted in J. Pavelek (ed.), *Gramatické dielo Antona Bernoláka* (Bratislava, 1964).

[13] Idem, *Grammatica Slavica* (Pressburg/Bratislava, 1790). Reprinted in Pavelek, op. cit. (n. 12).

(d) Croatian and Serbian

The repercussions of awakening Hungarian nationalism were also felt in Croatia, which had been subject to the Hungarian crown since the personal union of the two kingdoms in 1102. Since 1699 the territory of Croatia proper (Zagreb and the Zagorje) had been supplemented by the newly liberated Slavonia. Croats (using the term in the sense of all Catholic speakers of Serbo-Croatian dialects) also inhabited the Adriatic coast and islands, which in 1750 were still under Venetian rule. The Republic of Dubrovnik, which retained its independence longer than Venice, was also Croatian in language. There was no generally accepted written form of the Croatian vernacular, let alone any form of the language common to Croats and Serbs, whose speech was closely related and indeed in some areas almost identical. Literary dialects of relatively modest pretensions and local validity existed in Civil Croatia (especially Zagreb) and in Slavonia since the mid-eighteenth century. The literary language of Dubrovnik was of greater significance, though again only locally, and it no longer flourished as it had done in the sixteenth and seventeenth centuries. In Habsburg Croatia we find from at least the early eighteenth century similar developments of historical and antiquarian scholarship to those we have observed further north. The poet and historian Pavao Ritter (1652–1713), called Vitezović, drew attention to the Croatian national past in his historical work *Croatia rediviva* (Zagreb, 1700) and in a number of other works; and in his incomplete dictionary and in his reflections on his native language he uses the term *Croat* for all the southern Slavs. Of a different character, but illustrative of the growing interest in the national past, were the works of two Franciscans who worked partly or wholly in Venetian Dalmatia. Filip Grabovac (1697/8–1749) published in 1747 in Venice his miscellany of prose and verse narratives of past events in the South Slavonic territories and Albania.[14] Of more lasting significance was the collection of ballads made by Andrija Kačić Miošić (1704–60).[15] These were pastiches of popular ballads, generally with a historical content, composed in the traditional decasyllables of folk-poetry. Some of these found their way to the west in the Abbé Fortis's Italian translations and appeared among Herder's *Volkslieder*.[16]

In Habsburg Croatia the development of nationally oriented antiquarian, historical, and linguistic scholarship had somewhat lagged behind Dubrovnik, though here, too, interest in the vernacular had been evinced by a number of grammars and by the revival of literature in Slavonia under the influence of the educational reforms under

[14] F. Grabovac, *Cvit razgovora naroda i jezika iliričkoga aliti rvackoga* (Venice, 1747).
[15] A. Kačić Miošić, *Razgovor ugodni naroda slovinskoga* (Venice, 1756).
[16] J. G. von Herder (ed.), *Volkslieder*, i–ii (Leipzig, 1778–9).

Maria Theresa and Joseph II. It was in reaction to Hungarian pretensions that the language question came to the fore in Croatia. In the Diet of Buda in 1790 Hungarian deputies had demanded the introduction of Hungarian as the official language instead of Latin in Hungary and Croatia alike. These attempts were unsuccessful; but the Croats were prevailed upon to introduce the teaching of Hungarian into elementary and secondary schools in Croatia. From this time on the pressure of Hungarian grew ever stronger, and this pressure called forth an inevitable reaction among the Croats. The rights of the Croatian vernacular were invoked by the nobility, notably Count Janko Drašković in his message to the Croatian deputies at the Hungarian Diet of 1832,[17] and by a number of young intellectuals.[18] More than one of these writers mentioned the crucial problem that faced the Croats if they wished to raise their vernacular to the status of an all-purpose national language. This was the need to find a single, unitary form of the language to replace the disparate written dialects then in existence. Derkos spoke of a 'unification of the dialects of the three kingdoms [Croatia, Slavonia, and Dalmatia]'; Drašković, realizing that the local dialect of Zagreb was inadequate as a national language, wrote his memoir in a hybrid language which owed much to the literary dialect of Dubrovnik and other štokavic dialects. Such tendencies pointed the way to the solution of the Croatian language question, which was found by the publicist, writer, and politician Ljudevit Gaj, leader of what came to be known as the Illyrian Movement. Gaj, inspired by ideas of Slavonic kinship, sought to devise a common language for all the Southern Slavs—Croats, Serbs, Slovenes, and Bulgarians. He found it in the 'southern dialect', a form of štokavic strongly influenced by (though not identical with) the language of Dubrovnik. It is true, as has recently been pointed out by Croatian scholars, that the language devised by Gaj and his colleagues (notably the grammarian Babukić who codified the new language)[19] follows on naturally from earlier literary traditions and earlier ideas of what was the 'best' or most acceptable form of the Slavonic vernacular in the Croatian area. Nevertheless, it remains a remarkable and decisive fact in the development of the Croatian literary language that Gaj and his colleagues deliberately abandoned the existing literary dialects in favour of one which was not their own. It is also undeniable that this step resulted in large part from ideological considerations. Gaj did not succeed in imposing his chosen form of the vernacular on all the Southern Slavs; but it was sufficiently close to the form of language adopted by his great Serbian contemporary Vuk Karadžić to make it

---

[17] J. Drašković, *Disertacija iliti razgovor darovan gospodi poklisarom zakonskim* (Karlovac, 1832).
[18] e.g. I. Derkos, author of *Genius patriae super dormientibus suis filiis* (Zagreb, 1832).
[19] V. Babukić, *Osnova slovnice slavjanske narěčja ilirskoga* (Zagreb, 1836).

possible in the 1850s to speak for the first time of a Serbo-Croatian literary language. Vuk had turned away from the Church Slavonic which in unstable and hybrid forms had been the literary language of the Serbs in the eighteenth century and had codified a language based on the spoken dialects of Herzegovina and strongly influenced by the language of the traditional folk-ballads of the Serbs. In opting for the vernacular as opposed to Church Slavonic Vuk was following a trend already apparent among the Serbs of southern Hungary in the last decades of the eighteenth century. Nevertheless, his deliberate rejection of Church Slavonic, combined with his brilliantly simple reformed alphabet and his skilful grammatical codification, represents a decisive step which, alongside that of Gaj, opened up a new chapter in the linguistic history of his people.

(e) Rumanian (Transylvania)

We have seen how the emergence of Hungarian national sentiment and its expression in the language reform movement called forth a reaction among Slovaks and Croats. Yet another territory of the Hungarian Crown, Transylvania, was the scene of the first significant assertion of the linguistic identity of the Rumanians. In this province the Rumanians, though the most numerous nationality, occupied a status subordinate to that of the three ruling nations, Hungarians, Székely, and Saxons, who were represented in the Transylvanian Estates; and the Orthodox Church to which the Rumanians belonged was merely 'tolerated', unlike the 'received' Roman Catholic and Protestant (Calvinist, Lutheran, and Unitarian) faiths. As in Bohemia, the first phase of national revival was characterized by the scholarly examination of the national past. A series of talented scholars, almost all associated with the Uniat College at Blaj (Balázsfalva), were responsible for the first serious historical and philological studies of the Rumanians and their language. Samuil Micu-Clain (Klein) produced in 1780 the first modern Rumanian grammar in collaboration with Gh. Şincai.[20] Other grammatical and philological studies followed, and in 1812 Petru Maior published his historical study of the origins of the Rumanian nation.[21] All these works stressed the fact that the Rumanians were descendants of the ancient Romans and their language a corrupted form of Latin. The Roman origins of the Rumanian people had been asserted much earlier, for example by the seventeenth-century Moldavian chronicler Grigore Ureche ('. . . de la Rîm ne tragem').[22] But the Transylvanian scholars were not satisfied with the

[20] S. Micu-Clain (Klein), *Elementa linguae daco-romanae sive valachicae* (Vienna, 1780).

[21] P. Maior, *Istoria pentru începutul românilor in Dakia* (Buda, 1812).

[22] P. P. Panaitescu (ed.), Grigore Ureche, *Letopiseţul ţării Moldovei*, 2 ed. (Bucharest, 1958), 67.

establishment of this noble pedigree: they drew from it conclusions for the future development of their language. We are not concerned here with the details of the linguistic discussions that ensued, but only with the clear common purpose that emerged from it. It was necessary to purify the Latin vernacular of the Rumanians, to purge it of the non-Latin words that had entered it from Slavonic languages and Hungarian, and even (so some thought) to restore its phonological system to something closer to the Latin source. Although the forcible Latinization of the language was soon abandoned, the endeavour to transform the Rumanian language from a hybrid condition to a truly Romance language remained the constant preoccupation of scholars and writers; and this endeavour was soon taken up in the other Rumanian provinces, Wallachia and Moldavia, which were still ruled by Greek or Hellenized Rumanian princes under Turkish suzerainty. Thus a movement begun in Transylvania as a product of Enlightenment historicism and Josephine rationalism led in the course of the nineteenth century to a dramatic transformation of Rumanian under the influence first of Italian and then, more lastingly, of French.

(f) Slovene

To complete the picture of linguistic developments in the Habsburg domains we must turn back to the western ('Austrian') territories, to the Alpine provinces of Carniola (Krain), Carinthia (Kärnten), and Styria (Steiermark). Here German speakers were intermingled with speakers of the Slavonic dialects which we now call Slovene. German was the dominant, but not exclusive, language in the towns, notably Ljubljana (Laibach); but in the country districts there were extensive and compact areas of Slavonic speech. The Slavonic vernacular of Carniola had been committed to writing in the sixteenth century, as a result of the Protestant Reformation, in the Bible translations and liturgical and homiletic works of Primož Trubar and his associates and successors. However, the complete victory of the Counter-Reformation in the Austrian provinces brought about a decline in the use of Slovene for literary or, in general, written purposes from the seventeenth century onwards. A few devotional books and one reprint of a celebrated sixteenth-century grammar[23] were the sole printed specimens of Slovene in the first half of the eighteenth century. These works continued the tradition of Trubar's language, which was based on the dialects of Carniola. The Slovene dialects differ considerably from one another; and in German the language of Carniola, *krainisch*, was often regarded as something separate from that of Carinthia and Styria, *windisch*, a distinction which is also found in the works of some eighteenth-century Slovene writers.

[23] A. Bohorič, *Arcticae horulae succisivae de Latino-Carniolana literatura*, i–ii (Wittenberg, 1584).

The impact of the Theresan and Josephine reforms and of the development of historical study came to be felt from about the 1760s even among the Slovenes. Two grammars, that of Marko Pohlin[24] and that of Oswald Gutsmann,[25] were no doubt stimulated by Maria Theresa's educational reforms which, while encouraging the spread of German, also provided for elementary schools where instruction was in the local vernaculars. A further impulse for the use of Slovene in writing was provided by Joseph II's attempts to bring religion closer to the people, largely through greater use of the vernacular. To this we owe the new Slovene translation of the New Testament which appeared in 1784.

Just as in Bohemia the nobility had encouraged the scholarly study of the local history and language, so in Carniola the enlightened Baron Sigismund Zois provided the opportunity for young scholars to study and cultivate their native language. Prominent among them was Jernej (Bartholomäus) Kopitar. The result of Kopitar's researches was the first modern, scholarly grammar of Slovene.[26] This work gave an authoritative direction to the embryonic Slovene literary language. For the next three decades theoretical discussion of the form of the national language, and in particular its orthography, predominated over its actual use as a written medium. But, while these theoretical discussions mostly took place in German, poetry in the vernacular was much cultivated, and it is no exaggeration to say that it was the brilliant poetical achievement of Francè Prešeren (1800–49) in the 1830s that ensured the affirmation of Slovene as an independent literary language, despite the attempts of Gaj's Illyrian Movement to suppress it or at least subordinate it to Serbo-Croat.

(g) Estonian

The intellectual stimulus of the Enlightenment, particularly in its German expression, naturally made itself felt in the Baltic provinces of the Russian Empire which, until well into the nineteenth century, remained almost exclusively attached to the German cultural sphere in both literature and scholarship. Ideas of rationalism, tolerance, education, and exact scholarship affected the German intellectuals of Estonia and Livonia as they had those of the Habsburg dominions and caused them to direct their attention to the language and customs of their Estonian and Latvian serfs or parishioners. Probably the most important representative of these tendencies was August Wilhelm Hupel, a

---

[24] M. Pohlin, *Kraynska Grammatika, das ist: Die crainerische Grammatik, oder Kunst die crainerische Sprache regelrichtig zu reden, und zu schreiben* (Ljubljana, 1768).

[25] O. Gutsmann, *Windische Sprachlehre* (Klagenfurt, 1777).

[26] [J. Kopitar], *Grammatik der slavischen Sprache in Krain, Kärnten und Steyermark* (Ljubljana, 1808/9).

German-born clergyman who worked in Livonia for over thirty years and who produced a series of first-class scholarly works dealing with the Baltic provinces.[27] Interest in the Estonian language became widespread. Writers stressed the necessity of cultivating the language and of enabling the Estonians themselves, through better education, to use their own language to greater effect. The endeavours to this end were intensified and systematized in a scholarly journal—*Beiträge zur genauern Kenntniß der esthnischen Sprache*, edited by Johann Heinrich Rosenplänter and published in Pärnu (Pernau) 1813–32, and a learned society—'Ehstnische litterarische Gesellschaft', founded in 1817. Both were founded by Germans, but Estonians soon became associated with them. The grammarian O. W. Masing and the poet K. J. Peterson may be regarded as the first representatives of an Estonian educated class. Both began their literary activities in the second decade of the nineteenth century. Masing was in fact only half Estonian, his mother being Swedish, and his education was naturally almost exclusively in German. His influence on the development of the language, its orthography and grammar, can be compared with that of Dobrovský among the Czechs. Despite the gradual rise of an Estonian-born intelligentsia, Germans still continued for some decades to play a part in the fashioning of the Estonian literary language, at least in its scholarly codification, so that as late as 1884 it was possible for K. A. Hermann to claim with justice that he was the first investigator of the Estonian language to have grown up exclusively in Estonian linguistic surroundings. Nevertheless, the national literature made great strides, and when in the 1850s F. R. Kreutzwald composed the Estonian national epic *Kalevipoeg*, incorporating in it folk-poetry and many traditional Estonian myths and legends, the Estonian literary language had earned its place beside the older literary idioms of Europe. Nevertheless, the process of enrichment, stabilization, and standardization of the language, under the guiding influence of the related Finnish, continued until well into the twentieth century.

(h) Finnish

This language, too, had gone through a stage of purely scholarly cultivation, arising out of the antiquarianism and historical endeavours of the Enlightenment. At this stage the archaeological and ethnographic studies of H. G. Porthan (1739–1804) were of the greatest importance in making Finnish intellectuals aware of their national individuality and traditions. The next generation, after 1809 under Russian rule, was already fired by a nationalist fervour which was

---

[27] e.g. *Topographische Nachrichten von Lief- und Ehstland*, i–iii (Riga, 1774–82); *Ehstnische Sprachlehre für beide Hauptdialekte den revalschen und den dörptschen: nebst einem vollständigen Wörterbuch* (Riga–Leipzig, 1780).

forcibly expressed by Adolf Iwar Arwidsson. Arguing in favour of the rapid and intensive spread of education in the Finnish language he claimed language to be the fundamental element of nationality and the highest aim of the nation to be the retention of its individuality.

The Habsburg monarchy and the Baltic provinces belonged to what may be termed in the broadest sense the German cultural sphere; and we have seen how the revival of local languages drew much of its inspiration and practice from intellectual currents which flowed from or were mediated by German writers, thinkers, or institutions. Far different was the situation in the Ottoman Empire, in whose Balkan domains there lived European ethnic groups of the most disparate character: Serbs, Bulgarians, Albanians, Greeks, and Rumanians, to mention only the most numerous.

(i) Bulgarian

Among the Bulgarians literacy in the eighteenth century was largely restricted to the clergy. In monasteries writing was carried on in a somewhat Russianized Church Slavonic which was far removed from the spoken vernacular. In default of a native educated or ruling class national feeling was at a low ebb. Nevertheless, the rise of Russian power during the eighteenth century encouraged the revival of such feelings among all the Slavonic populations of Turkey; and western ideas of political democracy and intellectual freedom also began to penetrate into the Balkans, no doubt largely through the intermediary of educational institutions controlled by Greeks, such as the Athonite Academy, one of whose teachers, Eugenios Vulgaris, played an important part in transmitting French Enlightenment ideas to the Balkan world. It was in fact from Mount Athos that the first modern expression of Bulgarian national feeling emerged, though we do not know, indeed, whether its author was in any way directly inspired by the teachers of the Athonite Academy. The work in question was a treatise written in 1762 by Paisy, a monk of the Khilendar monastery on Mount Athos, and called by him *Slavyanobolgarskaya istoriya*. This purports to be a history of the Balkan Slavs, especially of the Bulgarians. Paisy was concerned to recall to his fellow-countrymen the glories of their medieval empires, to assert that their nation need not abase itself before Greeks and Turks, and to encourage pride in the native language. 'O Bulgarian,' he wrote, 'do not be deceived, know thy race and instruct thyself in thine own language.'[28] There are clearly parallels between the work of the Bulgarian monk and the historical writings of Slovaks or Czechs that have already been mentioned. Here too the scholarly examination of the national past leads to a preoccupation

[28] P. Dinekov (ed.), *Paisy Khilendarskii, Slavyanobǎlgarska istoriya* (Sofia, 1972), 41.

with the national language. Yet there is a great difference between Paisy's work and those works produced in the Habsburg monarchy. Whatever the shortcomings of the latter, they nevertheless display an awareness of the principles of critical historical study. (This is particularly true of the Bohemian writers.) Paisy, on the other hand, pieces together random information from a variety of sources, of different periods and unequal value, to produce an indiscriminate mixture of fact and legend. It is characteristic that even on such a matter as the ninth-century mission of Saints Cyril and Methodius, whose disciples played such an important part in the establishment and propagation of Christianity in Bulgaria, Paisy's account is based on corrupt and distorted sources. He does not seem to have known the Church Slavonic Lives of Saints Cyril and Methodius. Moreover, his main sources were secondary western ones, *Il regno degli Slavi* by the Dalmatian Mavro Orbini, and the *Annales ecclesiastici* of Cesare Baroni. Both these works had been written around 1600 and were known by Paisy in shortened Russian translations.[29] He found the first of these two texts, he tells us, in 'the German land': this would seem to refer to Sremski Karlovci in the Vojvodina (i.e. then southern Hungary), so that even his knowledge of the Russian translation came from the west. Yet the fact that the chief basis for Paisy's account of his nation's history was supplied by corrupt versions of outdated western works did not diminish its effect on his fellow-countrymen.

The language of Paisy's treatise is a curious and unsystematic hybrid of vernacular Bulgarian and Church Slavonic. Thus, neither in content nor in form could it serve as a reliable guide to those Bulgarians who in succeeding years undertook the revival of their nation and its language. This mattered little: the tone and spirit of the work were such as to make it a prime inspiration of Bulgarian national feeling. The fact that some 60 manuscript copies are preserved gives some impression of its popularity. It was more than fifty years after the composition of Paisy's *History* that the systematic movement to revive and reform the Bulgarian language got under way. It was intimately linked with the spread of education through the establishment of village schools and the work of itinerant teachers. Here too, then, we see the transition from the activity of the scholar to that of the practical language reformer; and here, too, important impulses came from the west.

(j) Rumanian (Moldavia and Wallachia)

In the two Rumanian principalities of Moldavia and Wallachia the level of secular education was higher than elsewhere in the Balkans, at least in the capitals of Jassy and Bucharest where 'princely academies'

---

[29] Ibid. 29.

(*academii domneşti*) had been established by the rulers already in the seventeenth century. It is true that the education in these institutions was almost entirely in Greek; but their importance lies in the fact that in them small, but not insignificant, numbers of Rumanian nobles received a humanistic education; and no doubt some of them became acquainted with works of the French Enlightenment in Greek translation. Thus, when in the 1820s ideas of national self-assertion made themselves felt in the Principalities and the question of the national language came to the fore, there were the makings of an intellectual class ready to form the new Rumanian literary language—under the strong influence of the ideas of the Transylvanian School.

(k) Greek

On the origins of the modern Greek literary language it must here suffice to say that this language differs from all those that have been discussed, for the simple reason that a form of classical or classicizing Greek had never ceased to be written. Diglossia had been the Greek linguistic condition from early Byzantine times: only the forms and conditions of that diglossia changed and, no doubt, are still changing today.[30]

I have concentrated so far on developments of the late eighteenth and early nineteenth centuries. By the 1860s all the languages discussed had attained a certain stability and were in regular use. There remain to be considered two languages which only achieved the status of literary languages in our own century—Albanian and Macedonian.

(l) Albanian

Scholars are not agreed as to the ultimate origins of Albanian, but so much is certain: that it is an Indo-European language, but forms a sub-group of its own, and that it had been spoken from early medieval times not only in the greater part of the territory of the present Albanian state, but had, by the nineteenth century, extended into parts of southern Serbia and Macedonia. Important Albanian colonies existed also in southern Italy and in Greece.

Among the Albanians of the Ottoman Empire no generally accepted form of the literary language had emerged by the end of the nineteenth century. Literary activity had been more in evidence among the Albanian diaspora in southern Italy. Divided in religion between Catholics, Orthodox, and Moslems, the Albanians of the Balkans were not even in agreement as to the alphabet they should use. Several systems based on the Latin alphabet were in competition with one another and with the Arabic script. The development of Albanian

[30] See R. Browning, *Medieval and Modern Greek* (1969).

national feeling after 1878 and the resulting oppressive measures of the Turkish authorities eventually led to a concentration of opinion in the alphabet question, which was vital if there was to be a common Albanian literary culture and unified educational practice. A high degree of agreement was reached at the Conference of Monastir (Bitola) in November 1908, when a representative gathering of Albanian intellectuals reached agreement on two alternative Latin-alphabet systems. One of these was the basis of the alphabet which predominated in independent Albania after 1918 and is now generally accepted. A unified alphabet, however, was not sufficient to solve the problems of the embryonic Albanian literary language. Tribal and cultural differences had brought about a very marked cleavage between two distinct dialect groups—the northern or Geg, and the southern or Tosk. It is only today that this problem is approaching a solution, now that Albanian scholars, supported by the authorities, have reached agreement on a modified form of Tosk.[31]

(m) Macedonian

The dialects of the neighbouring Macedonia were classed by most nineteenth-century scholars as Bulgarian dialects. Structurally, they do indeed follow the Bulgarian pattern, despite many local peculiarities. It is arguable that if the provisions of the Treaty of San Stefano in 1878 had been carried out and a greater Bulgaria had come into existence, embracing wide areas of the central Balkans including Macedonia, Bulgarian would have been accepted by the Macedonians as their literary language. The fact that the Congress of Berlin refused to allow the incorporation of Macedonia in the new Bulgarian state meant that this province had to wait until 1912 to be freed from Turkish rule. The separate development of Macedonia between 1878 and 1912 led to attempts to write in a language based on the local dialects. In 1903 Krste P. Misirkov in his work 'on Macedonian matters'[32] advocated such a language in precise and explicit terms. The fact that in 1913 liberated Macedonia was assigned to Serbia, and that this state of affairs continued after the formation of the Yugoslav state in 1918, delayed the independent national and linguistic development of Macedonia. But when, towards the end of the Second World War, the new federal Yugoslavia was established, the Macedonians were recognized as a separate nationality with their own language. The fact that this solution met with widespread acceptance and has led to the production of a flourishing and vigorous Macedonian literature would seem to justify the decision which in 1944 established Macedonian as the youngest European literary language.

[31] See G. Decsy, *Die linguistische Struktur Europas* (Wiesbaden, 1973), 117–19.
[32] K. P. Misirkov, *Za makedonskite raboti* (Sofia, 1903). Reprinted Skopje, 1953.

III. MEN, MOVEMENTS, AND MYTHS

We have seen how a new conception of language was formed throughout East-Central Europe, deriving ultimately from the intellectual developments of the eighteenth century, how it became a central element in the thinking of the era of Romanticism, and was responsible for the establishment of new literary languages, indeed standard languages, throughout the eastern marchlands of Europe. But movements of ideas and radical changes in linguistic practice are in the last resort the result of the activity of individuals. Adherents of a theory of historical determinism have argued that the influence of particular individuals on the processes of language reform was not decisive, that social and economic forces were moving in a certain direction so that the final result was inevitable: if one man or a certain group had not brought about the new national language, others would have done so. It may indeed be admitted that the social, political, and ideological conditions of the late eighteenth century were conducive to a rise in the status of national vernaculars. The rationalization of administration in the Habsburg domains inevitably raised the language question; the improvement of education created a new intelligentsia ready to question older ideas about the hierarchy of languages; ideas of political freedom easily extended from the freedom of the individual to that of national communities. The decline of the Ottoman Empire could not fail to inspire in the non-Moslem populations ideas of self-assertion which naturally took on a linguistic character. The scene was set for changes in attitudes to nationality and national languages. Yet at the same time it is certain that the new national languages would be other than they are, but for the deliberate and specific activities of certain talented and authoritative individuals. This is not the place to describe the details of the new languages as they were codified, propagated, and ultimately accepted in a particular form. I should like, however, to discuss some of those figures who in one way or another influenced the direction of linguistic evolution.

In the eighteenth century priests or monks predominated in the process of stimulating linguistic awareness and initiating linguistic change. In the western Habsburg provinces, particularly Bohemia and Slovenia, members of religious orders exercised a profound influence. The decline of the Jesuits, who had had a dominant influence in school and university education, enabled other orders to step into the breach. In Bohemia the role of the order of Piarists (Ordo Clericorum Regularium Pauperum Matris Dei Scholarum Piarum), a teaching order founded in 1618, was remarkable. Of the leaders both of antiquarian and historical research and of educational reform in that province from the 1750s onwards several were members of the Piarist order, notably

Gelasius Dobner who, in addition to the historical research that has already been noted, directed the Piarist College which had been founded in Prague in 1752. The order gained control of many schools in Bohemia, especially after the dissolution of the Jesuit Order in 1773; and in their educational practice they laid particular emphasis on the use of the vernacular, as against the Jesuit insistence on Latin. The dissolution of the Jesuit Order influenced the history of the Czech language in another, indirect, but highly significant way. Josef Dobrovský served his novitiate as a Jesuit, but was prevented from fulfilling his ambition to be a missionary in the Far East by the dissolution of the Order. Nevertheless, he was ordained priest and remained all his life a typical representative of the enlightened liberal Catholicism encouraged by Joseph II. In the new circumstances his attention gradually turned to his own language, with the results that have already been described.

In Slovenia members of various orders spread Josephine conceptions of religion and of the use of the vernacular for religious purposes: we have seen that the author of the first modern grammar of Slovene was the discalceate Augustinian Marko Pohlin. His successors in the first decades of the nineteenth century, writers of further grammars, were mostly parish priests.

An important stimulus to interest in the vernacular languages in the Habsburg monarchy was provided by the alumni of the General Seminaries (*Generalseminare*) instituted by Joseph II in many of the main centres of the monarchy. This was a move designed to remove the training of the clergy from the hands of the conservative bishops and to fashion the curriculum according to the monarch's own more liberal ideas. Great importance was attached to the vernaculars: the young priests were to be able to preach fluently and persuasively in the language of their parishioners. It is characteristic that Dobrovský was, for a few years, Director of the Moravian General Seminary at Hradisko, near Olomouc. The most remarkable instance of the direct influence of a product of the General Seminary system on the linguistic development is that of the Slovak Anton Bernolák, the author of the first grammar of the Slovak language.[33] Bernolák was the son of a peasant family from Orava in north-western Slovakia. Destined for the priesthood, he studied first at Trnava/Nagyszombat in western Slovakia, then in Vienna, and finally at the General Seminary of Bratislava/Pressburg, which had been established in 1784. We are reasonably well informed of the history and character of this institution. On 8 October 1784 the Emperor himself addressed the alumni, stressing among other things the importance of the vernacular. It is not too much to say that the first Slovak grammar is a product of the Pressburg

[33] See n. 13.

Generalseminar. Bernolák was one of a group of young Slovak priests from that institution who were fired with enthusiasm for the vernacular and grouped together in the 1780s (we do not know the exact date) to found the Slovak Learned Society ('Slovenské Učené Tovarišstvo'), with the aim of encouraging scholarly work in and on the vernacular. In 1787 Bernolák published his treatise on orthography, already mentioned; and in 1790 followed his grammar which, incidentally, was explicitly destined for schools in the Slovak-speaking regions of Hungary. Despite the fact that Bernolák's language, with its markedly western dialectal character, did not in the end form the basis of literary Slovak, it was he who first established the right of his native language to a place on the linguistic map of cultivated Europe. We may well doubt whether the history of the Slovak language would have developed as it did without the powerful incentive given by Joseph II through the General Seminaries. These institutions ceased to exist after Joseph's death in 1790, but they had played their part in the linguistic revolution in Central Europe.

Another group of priests whose activities in the study, revision, and propagation of their native language were closely linked with the Theresan and Josephine reforms were associated with the Uniat College at Blaj/Balázsfalva in Transylvania. The Uniat Church in Transylvania had come into being in 1698 through the acceptance of union with Rome by a large section of the local Rumanian Orthodox clergy. They retained the right to their own liturgy while accepting the essential doctrinal tenets of Catholicism, and thus became part of an 'accepted' rather than merely 'tolerated' religion and were able to enjoy the support and encouragement of the authorities. The Uniat College of Blaj commenced its activity in 1754, comprising a seminary, where Uniat priests were trained, and secular schools both elementary and secondary. The three scholars who were the leaders of the Transylvanian School, the 'Transylvanian triad'—Samuil Micu (Clain), Gheorghe Şincai, and Petru Maior—all taught at the seminary of Blaj; and their efforts to develop and propagate the Rumanian language followed on the Theresan *Ratio Educationis* (1777), which was extended to Transylvania in 1781.[34] Şincai and Maior had studied not only at Vienna but at the Collegium De Propaganda Fide in Rome. There they formed their conception of the Roman origins and affiliations of the Rumanian people and its language, to which they gave expression in their historical and linguistic writings.

In the Baltic provinces, too, the linguistic revival was first launched by the clergy. As has been noted already, the population of these provinces was for the most part Lutheran; and it was the Lutheran pastors, caring for Estonian and Latvian parishioners, who were responsible for the earliest writings in Estonian and Latvian. Most of them had

[34] See nn. 20–1.

studied in Germany and many had been born there. Their attitude to the vernacular languages in the seventeenth and eighteenth centuries seems to have been in the main a utilitarian one. It was their task, as they saw it, to bring the light of true religion to their ignorant and backward congregations. Their attitude was benevolent but condescending. Anton Thor Helle, the chief editor of the Estonian Bible translation made in the early eighteenth century, wrote, for example, in the preface to his Estonian grammar of 1732 that the chief aim of his book was to enable 'diejenigen, welche von Gott beruffen werden, diesem armen Land-Volck den Rath Gottes von ihrer Seligkeit zu verkündigen' to learn Estonian well enough to express God's will with greater emphasis and clarity.[35] Towards the end of the eighteenth century this attitude changed, under the influence of ideas of human rights and of the perfectibility of man. Men such as Hupel, Arvelius, and Rosenplänter combined local patriotism with a genuine altruistic concern for their Estonian fellow-countrymen. They wished to educate the Estonian peasants so that they would themselves reach the stage of cultivating their own language for literary and intellectual purposes. By the 1860s the new Estonian intellectual class had indeed begun to create a national literature and to take control of the nation's intellectual affairs. What modern Estonia has achieved in the cultivation of the national language and the elaboration of a fine literature, rich especially in poetry, would be unthinkable without the earlier efforts of the German Lutheran clergy. Much the same is true of Latvia.

In the Slavonic areas of the Balkans it was the monasteries which ensured the continuity of national culture; and we have seen how the monk Paisy, despite the handicaps imposed by the relative cultural isolation of the Ottoman Empire from Europe, was able to provide a stimulus and inspiration for the Bulgarian national and linguistic revival. Nor should it be forgotten that Dositej Obradović, the most eminent Serbian pioneer in the use of the vernacular, was a monk before he abandoned the religious calling to become an enthusiastic propagator of the ideas of the Enlightenment.

In the early, or scholarly period of national and linguistic revival an important part was played in the Habsburg territories by the nobility. We have already noted this factor in the case of Bohemia, where individual scholars were supported by aristocratic patrons. Here I would only add that Josef Dobrovský owed the leisure which was granted him to pursue his philological studies to the munificent patronage of Counts Nostitz, Czernin, and Sternberg, in whose houses he lived for several years. In Hungary, in contrast to Bohemia, it was the minor nobility that lent its support to the national movement. It was to this class, the

---

[35] A. T. Helle, *Kurtzgefaßte Anweisung zur ehstnischen Sprache* (Halle, 1732).

gentry, that Kazinczy belonged. It is, however, noteworthy that in Slovakia the gentry were hardly involved in the campaign for a national language, which was almost exclusively in the hands of the lower clergy and the new secular intelligentsia, almost all of humble origin.

In most regions of the monarchy this new secular intelligentsia was coming into existence. The process was linked with the complex growth of urban life, resulting from the beginnings of industrialization and the modernization of administration. The abolition or weakening of the system of serfdom meant that many sons of peasants, formerly tied to the soil, found their way to the towns, where it was easier to gain education and, for the more talented, to find employment in various educational and cultural vocations.

Let us examine rather more closely a few representative figures of this new generation. One of the most remarkable personalities, though perhaps not typical, was Vuk Stefanović Karadžić, the reformer of the Serbian literary language and the founder of the modern study of Serbian folklore and history.[36] Born in a poor peasant family, Vuk had no formal education apart from being taught to read and write by the monks of the Tronoša monastery in western Serbia. In the Serbian rebellion against the Turks of 1813 he was unfit for combatant service because of a leg ailment, but acted as clerk and secretary to one of the Serbian commanders. After the defeat of the rising he found his way to Vienna, where he was fortunate in meeting Kopitar, then librarian and censor at the Hofbibliothek. Kopitar immediately sensed the unusual talents of the Serbian youth and encouraged him to study the language and folklore of his people. The result, after a remarkably short space of time, was Vuk's grammar and dictionary of Serbian, incorporating his new orthography, and the beginnings of his collection of Serbian traditional ballads. Although he made frequent journeys to Serbia and other Balkan territories, Vuk resided in Vienna for the greater part of his life. This is one of the numerous examples of the importance of the imperial capital for the intellectual developments in all parts of the monarchy. Vienna was a magnet which drew to itself the talented youth of many provinces. Without this role of Vienna the meeting of Vuk and Kopitar, with its electrifying results for the linguistic history of the Serbs, could scarcely have taken place.

As chief librarian of the Hofbibliothek in Vienna and censor of Slavonic publications under the Metternich regime, Kopitar was a man of considerable influence. He was, moreover, a central figure in the polemical discussions which raged among the Slavs of the Austrian Empire concerning the shape and future of their literary languages. Here he was implacably opposed to the Illyrian Movement of the

---

[36] See D. Wilson, *The Life and Times of Vuk Stefan Karadžić, 1787–1864* (Oxford, 1970).

Croat Ljudevit Gaj. Gaj held the view, which he had formulated under the influence of the Slovak poet Kollár, that only four Slavonic vernaculars had the right to be cultivated as literary languages: Russian, Polish, Czechoslovak (in practice this meant Czech), and Illyrian (Serbo-Croat). Other Slavonic vernaculars might be used for local purposes, but must remain subordinate to the four 'principal dialects' (*Hauptdialekte*). In pursuit of this policy Gaj attempted to impose his version of the 'Illyrian' or Serbo-Croatian language on the Slovenes. This was not to the taste of Kopitar, not merely because, as a Slovene, he saw no reason to renounce or demote his mother tongue, but also because, as a staunch Catholic, he viewed with distaste and suspicion the activities of the Slovak and Czech Protestants, such as Kollár and Šafařík, who had influenced Gaj and his Illyrian Movement. Gaj himself he regarded, no doubt with justice, as a lapsed Catholic and free-thinker. One of the greatest of Gaj's misdeeds, in Kopitar's eyes, was that he had adopted for Serbo-Croat the Czech version of the Latin alphabet with its numerous diacritics. This he regarded as a vile Hussite invention: he referred to the diacritic marks as *stercora muscarum* ('fly-droppings'). Although Kopitar frequently expressed the wish that a 'new Cyril' should arise to devise a unitary orthography for all those Slavs who used the Latin alphabet, he refused to recognize that this role was in fact being played by Gaj: for in the end, owing largely to the activities of the Illyrian Movement, the Czech-style orthography was adopted by all the Slavs using the Latin alphabet except the Poles, who saw no reason to abandon their traditional spelling system.

By the 1830s the movement in favour of national languages was taking on political overtones. This is very clearly apparent in the life and work of L'udovít Štúr, the man who was chiefly responsible for establishing the Slovak literary language in the form which finally gained acceptance. Of humble origins, Štúr studied at the University of Halle and at the Protestant Lyceum (or College) at Bratislava/Pressburg. In 1843 he reached agreement with a group of colleagues on the principle that the Slovak literary language should be based on the central dialects of Slovakia instead of the western dialect favoured by Bernolák. In fulfilment of this decision Štúr published in 1846 a grammar of the new language and an eloquent and reasoned apologia for it.[37] Within little more than a decade the language established by Štúr was generally and finally accepted by his fellow-countrymen. But Štúr was no mere philologist. A journalist and public figure, he agitated powerfully for more rights for the Slovaks in Hungary, and took an active part in the revolutionary events of 1848. His political activities resulted in

---

[37] L'. Štúr, 'Náuka reči slovenskej' and 'Nárečie slovenské alebo potreba písania v tomto nárečí', in: *Slovenčina naša. Dielo v piatich zväzkoch*, v (Bratislava, 1957), 24–114, 153–253.

failure and disappointment; but his language has remained to the present day.

The writings and activities of most Slavonic intellectuals in the early nineteenth-century Habsburg Empire, of such men as Jungmann, Kollár, Kopitar, Gaj, and Štúr, whatever their differences of outlook, were in one way or another influenced by the view that they belonged to a single Slavonic race, speaking a single language which existed in separate dialects. Moreover, they believed that the Slavs could look back on an honourable and even glorious history in the period before they had been subjugated by the tyrannous Germans and the barbarous Hungarians. The present period of subjection, they believed, was nearing its end and would be followed by a period in which the Slavonic race would come into its own and advance towards a glorious future. This romantic vision was given poetic expression by the Slovak poet Jan Kollár (who, however, wrote in Czech and did not favour the movement for a separate Slovak language) in his lyrical epic *Slávy Dcera* (*The Daughter of Sláva*).[38] The prologue to this poem, composed in elegiac couplets, eloquently sets out the views I have just outlined. It has often been observed that this prologue reflects, sometimes in detail, the chapter in Herder's *Ideen zur Philosophie der Geschichte der Menschheit*[39] in which the German thinker painted an idealized picture of the Slavs. Although similar conceptions can be found in earlier writers, Slavonic and non-Slavonic, there is no doubt that Herder's chapter, with its enthusiastic and inspiring rhetoric, exercised a profound influence on the thought of all the Slavonic peoples of Central Europe from the moment of its publication in 1791.

The concept of the unity of the Slavs gave rise to a desire to manifest this unity in the form of a single language, which should replace the divergent existing languages and dialects. Some enthusiasts even tried to formulate the grammar of such a common language. Kollár, more practical in his approach to the problem, devised his doctrine of the four 'principal dialects'.[40] This reduction of the number of Slavonic literary vernaculars was to be the first stage of a process which would, in Kollár's conception, lead in time to the emergence of a single language, just as in ancient Greece earlier literary dialects had ultimately been replaced by the Attic *koiné*.

Such theoretical schemes could not withstand the force of local national feelings. The new Slovene and Slovak literary languages were not prepared to disappear even in the cause of Slavonic unity. Here

[38] J. Kollár, *Sláwy Dcera we třech zpěwjch* (Budin, 1824); *Sláwy Dcera. Lyricko-epická báseň w pěti zpěwjch* (Pešt, 1832).
[39] J. G. von Herder, *Ideen zur Philosophie der Geschichte der Menschheit*, pt. IV, bk. xvi, ch. 4, in: *Herders Sämmtliche Werke*, ed. B. Suphan, xiv (Berlin, 1909), 277–80.
[40] J. Kollár, 'O literárnej vzájemnosti mezi kmeny a nářečími slavskými', *Hronika*, i, No. 11 (Banská Bystrica, 1836).

the conservative Kopitar and the radical Štúr were at one. The conception of Slavonic peoples and languages linked by a common heritage, but each with its own individual and characteristic voice, was well expressed by Štúr: 'The life of the Slavs is multiform, like a linden-tree that has many branches; the nation is one, but its unity exists in diversity; may this diversity, then, reveal itself, though in unity, even in our intellectual life; may our intellectual life be based on our natural vitality, which is a result of our national variety (*kmenovitost'*), and thus life will be as it should be, set on good foundations, for nothing that should grow up will be choked and nothing will wither away.'[41]

The idealization of the Slavonic past was sometimes accompanied by interpretations or adjustments of history in senses favourable to particular nations. The Byzantine Greek scholar-missionaries, Saints Cyril and Methodius, who had created the oldest Slavonic literary language (Old Church Slavonic) in the ninth century, were transformed in Bulgarian popular belief into Bulgarians. For the Slovaks, however, they were the creators of the first literary language used by Slovaks—for the inhabitants of the Great Moravian Empire were held to be Slovaks. Moreover, the central Slovak dialects were declared by Štúr to be closest to the ancient language of the Slavs before their dispersal into their present territories. Slovene scholars, on the other hand, beginning with Kopitar, claimed Old Church Slavonic to be the ancestor of Slovene!

It was a similar desire to establish a noble ancestry for their nation and language, as we have already seen, which led the Rumanians to romanize their national tongue and to abolish or belittle those other elements in their linguistic tradition—Slavonic, Hungarian, Turkish, Greek—which in fact give added savour and character to the Rumanian language. This same tendency gave rise to the movement which in liberated Greece after 1830 favoured the classicizing *katharévousa*, despite the evident fact that the Greek ethnic make-up contains other elements than those that were present in Plato and Demosthenes.

Side by side with this historicizing tendency was the ideal of populism. The new languages were viewed as languages of the common people as opposed on the one hand to the alien languages of social superiors or political rulers, and on the other to the exclusive learned languages of the priests and scholars. This conception was at the root of Vuk Karadžić's outlook as well as that of Štúr; and we may note that in Greece the development of *dēmotikē* derives from the same romantic sentiment. The languages of the Estonians and Latvians were almost by definition languages of the common people and of those ruled, not ruling: both peoples were commonly designated as *Undeutsche*, and

41 Op. cit. (n. 37), 35.

the most usual term employed by the Estonians to describe themselves before the nineteenth century was *maarahva*, 'the country people'.

Here I must bring to an end this brief survey of the beliefs, true and false, and the ideologies, which guided the thoughts and actions of the leading figures in the language reform movement of East-Central Europe. From the point of view of the present-day observer many of these discussions may seem petty, even comic. Yet we must remember that these men were not dealing with language for its own sake. Here again, their attitude is well expressed in words addressed by Štúr to his Slovak fellow-countrymen in his apologia for the literary language which he introduced to them: 'And now we turn to you, Slovaks, and with hand on heart we say to you: everything we have done we have done and are doing for the life of the Slavs, for *your* life!'[42] Even minute questions of orthography reflected attitudes towards wider issues and were discussed with passion in the endeavour to find out what forms of expression most characteristically expressed the national individuality in the way in which it was conceived by the particular writer. Different conceptions led to conflicts; and conflicts were resolved, generally in ways that have stood the test of time.

As I said at the outset, the language movement developed into something wider, into various forms of political activity directed towards national self-assertion, and the map of Europe today—still more the map of Europe in 1921 or so—clearly shows some of the results of that activity. I have no wish to discuss these political consequences of the language movement, except only to say that regrets about what might have been if men had been more far-sighted or more rational are fruitless. The past is what it was; we cannot alter it. The task of the historian is to approach as close as he can to the always elusive realities of the past and to do so with what sympathy he can muster.

Yet, at the end of this all too summary survey it is perhaps proper to give some evaluation of the movement in East-Central Europe which I have described and which I regard as essentially one. I do not hesitate to say that, in terms of human values, my evaluation is a positive one. The variety of literary languages, not merely as vehicles of literature but as means of personal expression, has added new dimensions to the life of the mind in Europe; and the respect for these languages which derives from the memory of their precarious history is also something positive.

The Estonian poet Aleksis Rannit has recently said: 'The nineteenth and especially the twentieth centuries have been restoring, happily enough, the once destroyed Tower of Babel.' The image of the Tower of Babel was also invoked over a thousand years ago by St. Cyril and his

[42] Op. cit. (n. 37), 113.

disciples, when expressing their joy at the fact that the Slavs were now able to worship God in their own tongue: the curse of Babel, they said, had been superseded by the Pentecostal gift. The value of the language revivals of East-Central Europe lies in the fact that they have added immeasurably to the variety and quality of human experience and its expression.

Quintessential Saltykov:
Ubezhishche Monrepo

By I. P. FOOTE

THE publication of Saltykov's *Ubezhishche Monrepo* was completed a hundred years ago: it was serialized in *Otechestvennye zapiski* from August 1878 to November 1879.[1] This centenary provides a convenient pretext for examining *Ubezhishche Monrepo* and its place in Saltykov's work. It is a work which has not received much detailed attention in critical studies of Saltykov's writings.[2] Perhaps this is because it broaches no new subjects or because it poses fewer problems of interpretation than some other works of Saltykov: whatever the reason, its relative neglect has led to its being underrated and not recognized for what it is—a central and quintessential work in Saltykov's large and rambling opus. There is much to be said for being able to indicate one work which contains the essence of Saltykov. His literary and journalistic works fill seventeen volumes in the recent complete edition,[3] and much of what he wrote by way of commentary on his country and on his age is diffuse, elusive, and obscure. Individual works are best read in the context of all he had written before; to read them out of this larger context poses serious, sometimes insuperable problems of understanding. There are, though, important single works which can be taken on their own—and well-known works, such as *Gospoda Golovlevy*, *Istoriya odnogo goroda*, and *Poshekhonskaya starina*, are well known chiefly for this reason. *Ubezhishche Monrepo* is, in my view, also such a work and deserves to be better known.

I have called it central and quintessential. In what senses? It is central in a literal sense as having appeared half-way through the period from 1868 to 1889 (the year of his death), when Saltykov devoted himself full-time to literature. Although he had written a good deal before 1868, literature had been a secondary occupation in his

---

A paper read to the Study Group on Nineteenth-century Literature at its meeting in April 1978.

[1] The five parts appeared in *Otechestvennye zapiski*, 1878, viii, 1879, ii, viii, ix, xi. It was issued in book form in 1880.

[2] See, for example, Ya. El'sberg, *Saltykov-Shchedrin, zhizn' i tvorchestvo* (M., 1953), 422–34; V. Kirpotin, *Mikhail Evgrafovich Saltykov-Shchedrin*, izd. pererabotannoe (M., 1955), 402–6; K. Sanine, *Saltykov-Chtchédrine, sa vie et ses œuvres* (Paris, 1955), 235–42. There are significant references, but no systematic accounts of the work in A. S. Bushmin, *Satira Saltykova-Shchedrina* (M.–L., 1959) and E. Pokusaev, *Revolyutsionnaya satira Saltykova-Shchedrina* (M., 1963). Of the few articles on *Ubezhishche Monrepo* the only substantial one of general interest is S. N. Sokolov's 'Khudozhestvennye osobennosti *Ubezhishcha Monrepo* Saltykova-Shchedrina', *Uchenye zapiski Belgorodskogo gos. ped. instituta*, ii (1959).

[3] M. E. Saltykov-Shchedrin, *Sobranie sochinenii*, 20 vols. (M., 1965–77), hereafter *SS*.

life as a civil servant, except for the years 1862–4 when he worked
on *Sovremennik*. The period from 1868, when he became an editor
and regular contributor to *Otechestvennye zapiski*, was undoubtedly the
period of his maturity as a writer and as an interpreter of events. By
the time he wrote *Ubezhishche Monrepo* he was widely read and widely
respected, a writer who by his accurate observation of the Russian
scene and pungently written sketches evoked a response in a wide
section of educated Russians. He was also now restored to tolerable
health after the long illness which had kept him abroad for thirteen
months in 1875–6, and he had recovered the verve and zest for humorous writing which had for some time abandoned him.

 Ubezhishche Monrepo is, then, central in being a product of the
middle of Saltykov's mature period. It is quintessential in that it is
concerned with both the major themes—the social-political and the
social-economic—which are the subject of his thirty-years' commentary on Russia. It treats these themes in a balanced, economical fashion
as no other single work of his does. Other works may contain more
important and perhaps more striking statements on the political and
economic themes—*Istoriya odnogo goroda* and *Gospoda Golovlevy* come at
once to mind—but such works concentrate on one or other aspect and
lack the tidy comprehensiveness of *Ubezhishche Monrepo*. Its concentrated
form is also well suited to convey a quintessential view: it fills a mere
140 pages,[4] which makes it the shortest and most compact of Saltykov's
completed works (novels or sketch-cycles). And it is a work which
conveys well the stylistic flavour of Saltykov's satirical writing: the
main elements of his satiric method are to be found in it, used with
maximum skill and effect. It is the purpose of this paper to examine these
different aspects of *Ubezhishche Monrepo* and to demonstrate the interest
and importance of this too little regarded work.

 Ubezhishche Monrepo consists of five chapters. Each has a title:
'Obshchii obzor',[5] 'Trevogi i radosti v Monrepo', 'Monrepo-usypal'-
nitsa', 'Finis Monrepo', and 'Predosterezhenie'. The work appears to
have arisen from no previous total conception—this was not uncommon
for Saltykov: even *Gospoda Golovlevy* was created from parts not originally intended to form a coherent whole. The first chapter of *Ubezhishche
Monrepo* was prompted by Saltykov's experiences during the second
cold, wet summer he spent at Lebyazh'e, the country house on the
Gulf of Finland, which he had bought in 1877. It contains his reflections on the position and problems of the city-dwelling 'cultivated
man' (*kul'turnyi chelovek*) in retreat for a period in the country. He then
goes on to describe in detail the characteristics of the *kul'turnyi chelovek*—

---

[4] *SS*, xiii (1972), 265–404.
[5] In the journal edition entitled 'Ubezhishche Monrepo'; the present heading dates
from the book edition of 1880.

the cultivated member of the gentry, living on in some run-down property or else engaged in a professional or official capacity in the city: in either case he lacks social vitality and purpose and is a useless relic of the past and scorned as such by the rural community, particularly the merchants, kulaks, and tavern-keepers who since the Emancipation have inherited his economic and social position.

Having set out the situation of the *kul'turnyi chelovek* in general terms, Saltykov provides specific illustration of it in the three chapters 'Trevogi i radosti v Monrepo', 'Monrepo-usypal'nitsa', and 'Finis Monrepo'. These chapters have a clear narrative thread, and tell the story of the narrator (let us call him N) who suffers increasingly from the ambiguity and insecurity of his position in Monrepos; he is harassed, ridiculed, and threatened, and brought finally to liquidate his affairs in the country, sell his property to the local merchant Razuvaev, and flee with the purchase money to idle away his last years in less troublesome surroundings. In these chapters the political and social-economic themes are presented with great succinctness through the relationships of N with the local police-superintendent (*stanovoi pristav*) Gratsianov, and the merchant Razuvaev.

The final chapter, 'Predosterezhenie', is a warning addressed by Progorelov, an ex-landowner, to the new bourgeois elements of Russian society, whom he names in the chapter's dedication as the 'tavern-keepers, money-changers, entrepreneurs, railway builders, and other masters of the blood-sucking trades'. The warning is of the impermanence of their new-found dominance: Progorelov reminds them that they are only a transient feature of social history, just as the landowners had been when they—for some generations—were the dominant class. The warning is coupled with a plea to this bourgeoisie (as he calls them) to play their leading role in society with decency and concern, to maintain in deed the declared, but abused, principles of the age: 'property, family, and state'. Their activity could be wholesome and beneficial if they abandoned self-interest and made the mainspring of their lives love of country. It is with this plea for love of country that the work ends.[6]

---

[6] The relationship of Progorelov to the narrator of the chapters preceding 'Predosterezhenie' needs clarification. 'Predosterezhenie' stands outside the sequence of the 'Monrepos' theme (concluded in 'Finis Monrepo'), and it seems to have been first published—two months after 'Finis Monrepo'—as an independent sketch, being subsequently incorporated in *Ubezhishche Monrepo* for the book edition of 1880 (see the commentaries of R. Ivanov-Razumnik in M. E. Saltykov-Shchedrin, *Sochineniya*, iv (M.–L., 1927), 637, and V. A. Myslyakov in *SS*, xiii, 741). Though by class and situation related to the *kul'turnyi chelovek* narrator of the earlier chapters, Progorelov is temperamentally distinct from him. His entirely serious warning and appeal are similarly different in tone from the timorous ruminations of the *kul'turnyi chelovek* (significantly, the term *kul'turnyi chelovek* does not occur in 'Predosterezhenie'—there the landowners are referred to only as *propashchie lyudi*). It may also be noted that a landowner named Progorelov is referred to (in the third person) in 'Finis Monrepo', *SS*, xiii, 350. There

Ubezhishche Monrepo ends up as a compact and balanced whole: the first chapter (largely reflective) takes up the *kul'turnyi chelovek* and Monrepos theme, it is mainly a depiction of social psychology. The central three chapters (part dramatic, part reflective) 'tell the story', with the focus of interest shifting from N's relations with the authorities to his relations with the economic successor class. The final 'Warning' (again largely reflective) expands the theme of this class and states some positive ideals to be followed.

Ubezhishche Monrepo is told in the first person, with the *kul'turnyi chelovek* as the dominant, and Progorelov as the secondary narrator. Saltykov frequently employed the device of first-person narrative in his works, making the narrator serve as both object and medium of his satire. There are examples of this as early as *Gubernskie ocherki* (1856–7), and considerable use is made of the device in Saltykov's satires of the 1870s, notably in the novels *Dnevnik provintsiala v Peterburge* and *Sovremennaya idilliya*. The narrator in *Ubezhishche Monrepo* is, however, not limited to his own standpoint (the same is true of some other narrators): Saltykov in his own person reflects and judges and expresses his ideas in the discourse of the same narrator. It is rarely difficult to separate the two voices which share in the address to the reader, and the 'serious' and 'satiric' levels of narration are mostly distinct. At the same time, there is some affinity between Saltykov and his *kul'turnyi chelovek* narrator—not in character and outlook, but in social experience: the opening chapter with its references to the practical problems of estate management is largely based on Saltykov's own experiences as an amateur countryman in Vitenevo and Lebyazh'e, and in class and cultural background there is also a close relationship. It is an affinity which informs Saltykov's understanding and criticism of the *kul'turnyi chelovek*. In 'Predosterezhenie' Saltykov's voice is, of course, particularly clear.[7]

Let us now consider the way in which Saltykov explores his major

appear, therefore, to be good grounds for regarding N and Progorelov as two separate characters.

[7] V. A. Myslyakov in his perceptive study of the narrator in Saltykov's works draws attention to the stylistic advantage of a multi-voiced narrator. Referring to the use of contrast in satirical writing, he says:

> It is the element of contrast that gives rise to the complex figure of Saltykov's first-person narrator. The two opposing sides of this figure reflect the two mainsprings of satire—the ideal, which is its starting-point, and the world of evil, which is exposed in the light of this ideal. Besides this, the combination in the first-person narrator of the 'spirit' of a morally degraded (*poshlaya*) milieu and the world of the author's consciousness strikingly highlights the baseness of the one and the sublimity of the other. Shchedrin's 'I'-narrator is presented in the contrasting combination of the elevated and the base, the tragic and the comic.

(*Iskusstvo satiricheskogo povestvovaniya: problemy rasskazchika u Saltykova-Shchedrina* (Saratov' 1966), 106.)

themes in *Ubezhishche Monrepo* and how his treatment of them here relates to their treatment in his other works.

The political question preoccupied Saltykov throughout his career. The relationship of the state and its functionaries to the 'people' was repeatedly investigated by him from *Gubernskie ocherki* onwards. In *Istoriya odnogo goroda* (1869–70) Saltykov delivered his classic and definitive judgement on the Russian state. He saw the administration as an all-powerful, self-perpetuating oligarchy, which pursued purposes either harmful or irrelevant to those it administered; society was a perpetual victim, deprived of rights and loaded with duties. The town-governors of Glupov in *Istoriya odnogo goroda*, regardless of individual differences, 'all flogged the inhabitants', who were deemed to be always guilty of *something*. Saltykov's denunciation of the state was accompanied by criticism of the subservience and political immaturity of the people, who accepted the tyranny of such masters. Progress towards political and social well-being could only come, in Saltykov's view, when Russian society had grown out of its political infantilism and matured to a stage where it would be capable of contributing to life and demanding from it too.

The state theme recedes somewhat after *Istoriya odnogo goroda*, although in the 1870s it is continued in such works as *Gospoda Tashkenttsy* and *Pompadury i pompadurshi*. When Saltykov takes it up again in *Ubezhishche Monrepo*, we find the theme expanded to take account not only of the constant relationship of the state to society, but also of the actual political situation of the day. By the late 1870s political life in Russia had taken a new turn: serious initiatives were being taken against the established order, and a state of war existed between the government and the revolutionary groups who had turned to 'direct action'. In 1878 the terrorist campaign opened and in 1879 attempts were made on the life of Alexander II. It was just in this period that *Ubezhishche Monrepo* was written. The reaction of the state was to intensify control, to define clearly and simply the categories of those who were politically reliable and unreliable (*blagonamerennye* and *neblagonamerennye*), and to detect and suppress disaffection. It is the relationship of the individual to the authorities in *this* situation which constitutes the main theme of the chapter 'Trevogi i radosti v Monrepo'. The narrator, now of no fixed social position or occupation, a 'man of the 'forties' with something of a liberal past, yet also resentful for the 'affront' (*obida*) done to his class by the Emancipation, falls under suspicion and has to justify himself in the eyes of Gratsianov, the police officer newly appointed to his district.

Gratsianov is a police officer of a new style and a new function. He is contrasted with the old *stanovoi*, who was merely an ignorant and corrupt functionary. Gratsianov is sophisticated and intelligent, and he possesses the skill of reading men's hearts: he is a practitioner of *serdtsevedenie*. He is, in fact, an early literary portrayal of the modern political policeman. Not, though, that he should be taken merely as the portrait of a particular kind of state official. Gratsianov stands also for the administration as a whole. In 'Obshchii obzor' Saltykov refers to the *kul'turnyi chelovek*'s fear of the *stanovoi* and remarks parenthetically that the title *stanovoi* should not be taken in its literal sense:[8] his reference to the *stanovoi* in general and to Gratsianov in particular is a reference to the whole administration—a point that was not lost on the censor N. E. Lebedev, whose report caused 'Trevogi i radosti v Monrepo' to be rejected when first put forward for publication in November 1878: 'Shchedrin makes use of a well-known literary device employed when persons and things cannot be referred to by their proper names, and one has to express oneself allegorically: he very skilfully compresses the actions and dispositions of the administration into the narrow framework of the *stanovoi*.'[9]

There is a twentieth-century ring about the criteria by which the political reliability of a person is assessed. To be deemed unreliable and subjected to suppression requires no overt act, only the inference by the authorities that you may hold such and such an opinion. Nonconformity of any kind—reading books, keeping to oneself, incautious use of dangerous words (such as *svoboda*)—can lead to one being considered a sympathizer (*sochuvstvovatel'*) with revolution—*factual* evidence is not required, only the conviction of the authorities that a person is guilty. The result of this in society is a mood of uncertainty and apprehension, a tendency for ordinary people to live with bated breath, awaiting retribution for uncommitted, undefined political crimes. 'Somehow', says N, 'I suddenly felt that they could do whatever they liked with me—throw me into gaol, turn me inside out, grind me to powder. Of course, having first convicted me of treason, which—if you have the facility for reading people's hearts—presents no serious problem.'[10] It is only in certain respects that Saltykov is a 'dated' writer.

N's feeling in general is to look back nostalgically to the rigid old regime of Nicholas I: then it was marching for everybody without question, but at least you knew where you were. It was in many ways preferable to the uncertainty and arbitrariness of the present, when you have no idea whether the authorities will deem you to belong to the reliable or the unreliable category.[11]

[8] *SS*, xiii, 283.
[9] Quoted in V. E. Evgen'ev-Maksimov, *V tiskakh reaktsii: k stoletiyu rozhdeniya M. E. Saltykova-Shchedrina* (M.–L., 1926), 66.
[10] *SS*, xiii, 297.
[11] Ibid. 301. Cf. the similar comparison of the two periods made by Turgenev in a letter to A. S. Suvorin of 14/26 Feb. 1875: 'The time we are living in is beastlier than that of our youth. Then we stood before a tightly closed door; now the door seems to be ajar, but to pass

The administrative philosophy of Gratsianov is characteristic of the totalitarian state. His aim is to make the populace industrious and faithful instruments for carrying out the designs of the authorities. Society, that is, exists for the state, not the state for society. His method of control is set out in a speech he delivers to an assembly of *uryadniki*.[12] The speech was in fact a blatant parody of a speech made shortly before (October 1878) by the governor (*gradonachal'nik*) of Odessa, General A. K. Geins, to the city police—the connection was also noted by the censor Lebedev.[13] In this speech Gratsianov instructs the *uryadniki* in their duty to maintain the existing order and destroy its enemies. Their prime task is to learn everything about everybody in their district and in the light of this knowledge take steps to eliminate disaffection. The method proposed for acquiring such knowledge is a universal network of spies and informers.

Gratsianov represents the tyranny of the state in its insidious modern form, which extends its power into the inner lives of its citizens. N responds with the customary spirit—or lack of spirit—of the citizens of Glupov. From childhood he has gone in fear of the authorities (*u menya voobrazhenie napugano nachal'stvom*); he is inclined to accept the official assumption that he, like any other citizen, must be guilty of *something*. Gratsianov's arrival throws him into panic: he fears the *stanovoi* will read his heart and find every kind of unwholesomeness. He protests to himself that he has done nothing wrong, that there is no law against dying or having no occupation—but, in making this protest, he is acknowledging the possibility, even the validity, of an official point of view which *may* condemn him for dying or doing nothing. When Gratsianov plants a spy in his house—an unknown man turns up and sleeps in his kitchen—N complains, but not of the spy's presence, only of the disturbance he creates by playing the accordion. N will always surrender to authority. In an ironically ecstatic scene he opens his heart for Gratsianov to read, confesses to having supported the reforms, shown concern for the peasants, and deplored their exploiters; he confesses circumspectly and is careful to avoid making any protest about the situation of himself and his class in the new times. He is, though, finally led on by Gratsianov to express himself openly on this question and he does then give way to the resentment felt by his class at the 'affront' of the Emancipation, the loss of their rights and privileges as landowners. But still he emphasizes that he is still not *protesting*, for it is not in his nature or the nature of his class to protest. The 'fig in

through it is more difficult than ever.' (I. S. Turgenev, *Polnoe sobranie sochinenii, Pis'ma*, xi (M.–L., 1966), 26.)

[12] *Uryadniki* were police agents first appointed in 1878, chiefly for the purpose of tightening political control in the provinces. They were particularly charged with keeping watch for 'activities and agitation directed against the government, lawful authority, and public order'.

[13] Evgen'ev-Maksimov, op. cit. (n. 9), 67.

the pocket' (*kukish v karmane*)—a variant of the Russian tradition of *bunt na kolenyakh*—is as far as he would ever go in opposition to the authorities.

In the political stance of N, Saltykov is not only criticizing the common Russian predisposition to submit to authority, he is also striking a characteristic blow at the compromising nature of the Russian liberal. Condemnation of the liberals figures prominently in Saltykov's writings: in the 1860s he attacked the pseudo-liberals who adopted reformist attitudes when reform was officially favoured; later, the 'sincere' liberals were no less an object of attack. They were ridiculed and damned by him throughout the 1870s for their gradualist policies and feeble compromise in the face of government reaction. N is a social rather than a political type, but in many ways he can be seen as a representative of gentry liberalism—he is a man of culture, conscience, and humane disposition, a one-time adherent of the idealism of the 1840s. Yet, with this intellectual attachment to liberal, humane ideas there went a lack of real commitment to a political cause and also an inbred attachment to one's own class privileges—a dichotomy summed up in the splendid opening of Saltykov's sketch 'Kul'turnaya toska' (1875): 'I was sitting at home and could not think what to do with myself. I wanted something—but could not decide whether it was a constitution, *sevryuga* with horse-radish, or to give someone a flogging.'[14] Progorelov recalls a similar paradox when, in his earlier years, he would attend a lecture given by Granovsky and then go off to conclude a deal for the sale of serfs. In *Dnevnik provintsiala v Peterburge* Saltykov had summed up the liberals as 'cream-skimmers' (*penkosnimateli*)—an indication both of the superficiality of their approach to problems and of their material enjoyment of a privileged station in life. Both aspects of liberalism—its gradualism and its spinelessness—are reflected in N's explanation to Gratsianov. The reprehensible past opinions to which he confesses are moderate indeed: he had favoured the reform initiatives of the government in the 1860s, and he had hoped that the Emancipation would cause the peasant promptly to feel some difference in his lot (but the landowner as little difference as possible). The attack on N's ideals and his submissiveness to the authorities parallels Saltykov's criticism of the liberals. The message is the same: to be humane and well-meaning within the bounds of convenience and self-interest is worthless; commitment and self-sacrifice are necessary if social and political progress is to be made.

So much then for the political questions touched on in *Ubezhishche Monrepo*. The main points of Saltykov's criticism of Russian political life are made. On the matter of state–society relations it looks back to *Gubernskie ocherki, Satiry v proze, Istoriya odnogo goroda,* and *Pompadury i*

---

[14] *SS*, xii, 295.

pompadurshi, which attack the tyranny of the state; it also stands with *Sovremennaya idilliya*, *Pis'ma k teten'ke*, and other later works in its reference to the crisis of state and society at the time when it was written. If it does not contain any direct or detailed indictment of post-reform liberalism, still an attack on liberal triviality and pusillanimity is subsumed in Saltykov's presentation of the *kul'turnyi chelovek* and his relations with the authorities.

The political theme is stated chiefly in one chapter, 'Trevogi i radosti v Monrepo'; the social-economic theme is explored at greater length and runs through the whole book.

Despite the shift in Russian economic life towards industrialization and urbanization in Saltykov's time, he devoted relatively little attention to it in his works. The economy was still primarily agricultural, and Saltykov's focus of interest was always the countryside. From the 1860s he traced the course of Russian rural life as it developed in the years following the Emancipation. By the 1870s the new pattern of society had emerged. Three groups were involved: first, the old land-owning class, largely a spent force, unable to cope with the new conditions and the problems of management without a tied labour force; secondly, the rising dominant class made up of merchants, prosperous peasants, and various kinds of entrepreneurs, not all of them home-bred—Saltykov frequently refers to the 'predators of various races' (*raznoplemennye khishchniki*), Jews, Greeks, and Germans, who buy up former gentry properties; thirdly, there was the peasantry—the agricultural base, providers of the labour on which the prosperity of the successive classes of property-owners was founded.

This social triangle, or separate points of it, provides a constant and dominant theme through most of Saltykov's *Otechestvennye zapiski* period, especially in *Dnevnik provintsiala v Peterburge*, *Blagonamerennye rechi* and its offshoot *Gospoda Golovlevy*, *Za rubezhom*, and the *Skazki*. *Ubezhishche Monrepo*'s claim to be quintessential depends not least on the fact that it provides the most succinct and clearly defined statement of the condition of Russian society. As *Istoriya odnogo goroda* can be regarded as the summary statement of the social-political theme, so *Ubezhishche Monrepo* might be regarded as the crystallization of the social-economic theme.

Saltykov employs two representative figures in his analysis of rural society: the *kul'turnyi chelovek* narrator and the merchant Razuvaev— both of them incidentally excellent examples of Saltykov's ability to represent in an individual the whole history and psychology of a class.

The *kul'turnyi chelovek* is the more complex portrait. Apart from the ambiguity which stems from the different tones of his narrative— some his own, some clearly Saltykov's—the character is complex in himself. There is much subtlety in Saltykov's account of him, which can be rated as one of his best achievements in the field of social-psychological portrayal (one might note that it is roughly contemporaneous with his final work on Porfiry Golovlev, who probably represents the height of Saltykov's psychological characterization).[15]

The idle or trivially engaged members of the privileged classes had come under Saltykov's scrutiny in the 1860s. He had taken them up again more recently, notably in the incomplete cycle entitled *Kul'-turnye lyudi* (1875–6) and in the sketch 'Dvoryanskaya khandra', published in January 1878, a few months before the first chapter of *Ubezhishche Monrepo* and a direct forerunner of it. The label '*kul'-turnyi chelovek*' stems from the 1875–6 cycle. There are some shifts of emphasis between 1875 and 1878, but the basic characteristics are the same: the *kul'turnye lyudi* are *passé*, superfluous, lacking any defined social function, fit only for a leisured existence, mildly decadent. In *Ubezhishche Monrepo* the type is presented with what appears to be a good deal more sympathy than in the earlier sketches—partly because of the first-person narrative, partly because the *kul'turnyi chelovek* appears in better light than his tormentors Gratsianov and Razuvaev. Essentially, however, the portrait is critical.

The narrator is presented in terms of self-deprecating irony: he is a man of leisure, unpractical, aesthetically inclined, whose presence in the country has only a therapeutic purpose:

> The cultivated man is in general a person who enjoys a considerable amount of leisure, has a fairly clear idea of the comforts and conveniences of life, is fond of taking off into the realms of aesthetics and speculative thought, but is rarely endowed with any practical knowledge. . . . Field cultivation is not for him, he needs only a view of the fields. He needs walks, relaxation, plenty of air, freedom from excitement, a carefree existence. . . . It is not labour he seeks in the country, but an untroubled vegetable existence to counteract the richness of life in town.[16]

He is a man on the retreat from life—symbolized in his search for a *refuge* in Monrepos. It is an interesting reflection of the change in social conditions that the gentry nests of an earlier period tend to be springboards—albeit rather flaccid ones—for excursions into the wide world (even Oblomovka was that), but the nest in Saltykov's works of the 1870s is a refuge *from* the world, a bolt-hole and a place in which to die—'Monrepo-usypal'nitsa', or Golovlevo as a tomb for the home-coming members of that family.

We see the narrator, after his initial self-characterization, in two relationships—with Gratsianov and with Razuvaev, the political and

---

[15] The final chapter of *Gospoda Golovlevy*, 'Raschet', was published in May 1880. The ending of the novel preoccupied Saltykov for a considerable time before this.

[16] *SS*, xiii, 270–1.

the social. In the political context the *kul'turnyi chelovek* is abject, pusil-
lanimous. In the social context he has more dignity. Economic history
is against him, and he concedes his old position to the Razuvaevs, but
he does so grudgingly. Social pride is a distinct feature of the *kul'turnyi
chelovek*—and his 'culture', however trivial its manifestations, is better
than the brutishness which characterizes the new pillars of society.
Driven beyond endurance by the crude familiarities of Prokhorov (one
of Razuvaev's associates), he spits in his face, and when Razuvaev
thrusts a wad of banknotes at him as an offer for Monrepos, he shows
him the door. He is sensitive to the barbarity of exploitation which the
rule of the Razuvaevs brings. He is also sensitive to his own situation.
Though not a protestor, he is reasonably resentful that—subjected to
the familiarities of Prokhorov, the suspicions of Gratsianov, the harass-
ment of Razuvaev, and the neglect of his remaining servants—he is not
allowed to die in peace, which is all he wants. He acknowledges that as
a social force he is finished, but he cannot help it if he happens still to be
alive. As for the past, he accepts no special responsibility; he enjoyed
legal rights and privileges which were, he agrees, immoral, but they
were part of the established order of things and ordinary men who had
been brought up in their enjoyment accepted them. Only exceptional
people were fit for the heroism of renunciation. In many ways this is
a reasonable claim for understanding of the limitations of ordinary
human beings caught up in a situation which they themselves had not
created. But its validity is not accepted by Saltykov. In Progorelov's
'Warning' he counters directly the self-justifying arguments of the
kul'turnyi chelovek. Progorelov—whose tone, of course, is not that of the
self-deprecating ironist, but of a repentant nobleman and impassioned
patriot—points precisely to the moral weakness of the landowning
class as a cause for their now being ruined (*propashchie lyudi*): because
they led ordinary complacent lives, because they compromised with their
consciences—accepting the privileges of their class without any thought
of social justice—they have deserved their fate.[17] Here, through Progorelov, Saltykov preaches a doctrine of moral responsibility.

One thing Saltykov is prepared to grant in favour of the *kul'turnyi
chelovek*, however, and that is that he is preferable to Razuvaev: 'I don't
know what other people think, but in my view, if circumstances offer
no other choice than to be a feebling or a blood-sucker, it is still more
decent to be a feebling.'[18]

There is no ambiguity in Saltykov's presentation of Razuvaev.
He had sketched the type already in *Blagonamerennye rechi*; there he
described the rise to wealth and social status of Derunov, once a small-
time dealer and now the local magnate. He, like Razuvaev in *Ubezhishche Monrepo*, becomes the purchaser of the narrator's estate. Derunov

[17] *SS*, xiii, 397–8.   [18] Ibid. 363.

is more amiable than Razuvaev, but both belong to that mixed body of predators who rose to the surface after the Emancipation—possessed of 'clear heads, sharp eyes, and strong nerves', they are acquisitive, ruthless, socially irresponsible, and *un*cultivated. These *chumazye*, as Saltykov labels them, are the new possessor class, to whom history for a time belongs. It is they who are now accepted and approved by the authorities as the new pillars of society, and Saltykov reflects on the irony of society's principles of 'property, family, and state' depending for support on a gang of self-interested, adulterous expropriators.

The *chumazye* are dynamic, but they are destructive, not productive. They are not planners or husbandmen; they exploit natural resources without thought for the future, and as exploiters of the peasantry they open up undreamt-of horizons: when the narrator remonstrates with Razuvaev that to deprive the peasant too thoroughly will leave him with nothing more to be deprived of, Razuvaev's reply is 'He'll find something' ('*ien dosta-a-nit*'). As Saltykov remarks, he has destroyed the legend of the goose that laid the golden eggs—Razuvaev will go on extracting eggs after he has cooked the goose and eaten it.[19]

As well as his destructiveness, it is the brutish vulgarity and insensitivity of Razuvaev which is so alarming. He is contrasted with the bourgeoisie of western European countries, who have achieved social power through patient industry and the exercise of productive skills, and have contributed to the social and cultural life of their countries. Progorelov's 'Warning' paints a frightening picture of the continuing onward march of the Razuvaevs—of the establishment of their uncouth rule, the destruction of natural and human resources, and the degradation of any kind of decent, principled life by the *chumazye*, whose conception of 'truth' is summed up in the phrase of the tavern sign '*raspivochno i na vynos*'.

The third element of rural society—the peasantry—is represented by no single character in *Ubezhishche Monrepo*, but the group figure of the *seryi chelovek* is continually in the background. Actual treatment of the peasant question in its various aspects—social, economic, cultural— takes up considerably less space in Saltykov's works than his treatment of the more conscious levels of society. Yet the peasant question was *the* central one for Russia—the whole future depended on its resolution. So, in *Ubezhishche Monrepo*, although the possessor classes are given most attention, the peasants are clearly indicated as the economic base of the country, without which the *kul'turnyi chelovek* and the Razuvaevs could neither prosper nor survive. In the opening chapter Saltykov recalls—obviously in his own voice—that he grew up in a *pomeshchik* household aware that the cup of life was full, but unaware of 'that fearful mass of effort, physical toil, exhaustion, sweat, murmuring,

[19] Ibid. 372.

and despair that went to fill the cup'.[20] Saltykov did not idealize the peasants; far from it, he saw them in real terms. In *Ubezhishche Monrepo* negative features of the peasants are not concealed—they are conservative, cunning, unwilling, they overrun the landowners' boundaries, pilfer his vegetables, and steal his wood (incidentally, Saltykov's correspondence with A. F. Kablukov, who acted as his agent at Vitenevo—Saltykov's former estate near Moscow—contain numerous complaints of this kind against the local peasantry).[21] They are passive, and unaware of their own interests: they fall ready victims to the bondage of the tavern, and though they dislike and will suffer from Razuvaev, they accept him and his dominance as inevitable.

But, for all their faults and weaknesses, the peasants lead a life governed by its own logic—the struggle against nature to produce a livelihood from the soil. At every point the peasant is shown to be the superior of the *kul'turnyi chelovek*. His life makes sense. He works hard, he is resourceful, he achieves by toil what the landowner can never achieve by agricultural theory. In domestic life, too, it is the peasant who has the skill, who serves, and who provides. The *kul'turnyi chelovek*, like Oblomov, is incapable of fending for himself in the simplest matters of life. He complains of the neglect of his servants, but he also recognizes that worse than their present neglect is the knowledge that the servant has only to realize that he is superior to his master for his service to stop altogether:[22] it is the old theme of Saltykov's best-known fable 'Povest' o tom, kak odin muzhik dvukh generalov prokormil'.

Transformation of Russia can only come through a transformation of the peasantry. In a remarkable passage in 'Monrepo-usypal'nitsa' N, day-dreaming, foresees a future happy Russia founded simply on a well-fed peasantry: all that is needed for a contented Russia is '*chtoby muzhik russkii "el dobry shchi i pivo pil"*'. If the peasant can enjoy only a fair share of the fruits of his toil, then Russia will be transformed—production will rise, state revenues increase, exports flourish, social and cultural benefits will flow. The peasant will cease to be a beast of burden and become a rational being. The social change would abolish the major problems of Russia—and by implication political changes would follow.[23] This is in 'Monrepo-usypal'nitsa' only a day-dream, but it is a substantial statement of a persistent belief of Saltykov—the mechanics of the change are not part of the dream but, as we shall see, some indication of the broad ways to be followed is given in a number of significant passages of *Ubezhishche Monrepo*.

[20] *SS*, xiii, 267.
[21] These letters, written over the period 1867–77, are in *SS*, xviii(1–2), xix(1).
[22] *SS*, xiii, 361–2.
[23] Ibid. 336–7.

As a critical and satirical writer Saltykov was primarily concerned with the negative aspects of life. The positive ideals he supported have to be deduced as best they can, and in necessarily general terms, from the line of his attack. However, from time to time he declares himself more openly, and *Ubezhishche Monrepo* stands out for the extent to which Saltykov states ideals and defines positive aims. These statements are made chiefly in the first and last, non-narrative, chapters. He makes two positive demands—for 'social concern' and for 'love of country'. Both are made to the possessor classes and require from them a renunciation of the self-interest and indifference which have characterized them in the past.

Saltykov first touches on the need for and the possibility of social involvement in the opening chapter. For the *kul'turnyi chelovek* to live idly in the country is shameful—he could, for instance, concern himself with the peasant, give him advice, help, and instruction. However inferior in practical matters, the *kul'turnyi chelovek* has still the advantage of education, and should take on the task of enlightenment: 'To give a man understanding of the fact that he is a man . . ., to open to him the possibility of distinguishing justice from injustice . . .', these are the worthy tasks which could be undertaken—but generally are not, for fear of what the authorities might think.[24]

The theme of social concern is taken up again in Progorelov's 'Warning'. It is stated in the passage where Progorelov points to the landowners' past lack of moral responsibility as a reason for their present ruin. They had shown no concern for the unjust social order which gave them their privileges, and even when aware of the unfair social distinctions they made no protest. The requirement here is clear: to be socially *conscious*, to understand one's society, and to be positive in correcting its injustices—by helping the needy and by raising one's voice in protest. It is implied here, as it was stated in the earlier 'social concern' passage, that this is a demand which can reasonably be fulfilled by ordinary people, indeed it must above all be fulfilled by ordinary people, for effective social change can only come from a change of outlook and behaviour on the part of the majority.

This plea for social involvement relates not only to the past of the gentry and the present of the rising bourgeoisie. It had a particular relevance, too, for the public at large in the political situation when Saltykov was writing *Ubezhishche Monrepo*. It can be read as a call to turn from political as well as social indifferentism, to face and not to flee the issues of the day. This call had been sounded in Saltykov's recently completed cycle *V srede umerennosti i akkuratnosti*, and it was reiterated in works which followed *Ubezhishche Monrepo*, such as *Pis'ma k teten'ke* and certain of the *Skazki* (e.g. 'Premudryi piskar''): civic

[24] Ibid. 282.

heroism may be beyond the capacity of the average man, but civic responsibility is not and it should be accepted.

The demand for concern in relation to society is only part of the larger demand for dedication to the interests of one's country as a whole.

The theme of country (*otechestvo*) is first mentioned in 'Monrepo-usypal'nitsa'. At a certain point Saltykov abandons the ironic stance of the *kul' turnyi chelovek* in order to refute accusations of his critics that he wrote too negatively about Russia and lacked patriotism. His answer is a curious and passionate declaration of love:

> I love Russia with a love which makes my heart ache. . . . I cannot even imagine myself anywhere but in Russia. . . . Only once have I had occasion to spend any length of time in the salubrious airs of foreign parts and I do not recall a minute when my heart was not yearning for Russia. It is fine abroad, and—let us admit it—it may not be so fine with us at home, . . . but still it turns out that at home it is actually better. It is better, because it hurts more.[25]

This declaration is turned in the final section of the work into a demand by Progorelov that the Razuvaevs should before all else love their *country*. If one cares about Russia, then the foundations of happiness and social justice will be laid. The evils of Russia stem from selfishness and indifference; both 'official' and 'social' Russia should place country before self—other problems will then solve themselves. The last words of *Ubezhishche Monrepo* are: 'And still the most important thing is: love, love, love your country. For this love will give you the strength to accomplish without difficulty all other things.'[26]

Besides these declarations of aims, there are in *Ubezhishche Monrepo* other statements by Saltykov which are of interest for an understanding of his view of life. In general, Saltykov never abandoned the Utopian vision of a bright future which he had entertained in the 1840s. His awareness of the corruption and distortions of life went together with a remarkably resilient belief that in the end reason, decency, and justice would prevail. This optimism for the future breaks through from time to time in his works, though perhaps not often enough to dispel the overall gloomy impression created by his portrayal of human vice, selfishness, folly, and falsehood.

There are, for instance, indications in *Ubezhishche Monrepo* of his views on historical progress and the development of societies. These come in Progorelov's 'Warning' and relate to the Razuvaev stage in the social-economic development of Russia. It is a period, says Progorelov/Saltykov, which has come about gradually and still has to reach its climax, but in time the Razuvaevs—like the gentry they succeed—will in their turn become *propashchie lyudi*. What might follow the

²⁵ *SS*, xiii, 334.   ²⁶ Ibid. 404.

Razuvaev stage is not stated, but a couple of hints are thrown out—
one in the reminder to Razuvaev that the brothel-keeper Rotozeev is
waiting to step into his shoes (a fate for Russia even worse, presumably, than the rule of Razuvaev), the other in the warning to Razuvaev
that he has come to the top in an age of confusion and instability, and
that the morsel he now holds may be snatched from his hands—the
passage is cryptic: perhaps Saltykov is referring to the jungle state of
society in which even the predator may become the prey, or he may be
suggesting the possibility of a revolution which would dispossess the
possessors—though doubtless, in Saltykov's view, such a revolution
would be prompted by elemental need rather than by political pro-
gramme. The idea of progress occurs also in relation to the history of
social classes. They, too, are not static. In recording the decline of the
pomeshchik class Saltykov was chiefly concerned with class degeneration,
apparently complete by the time of *Ubezhishche Monrepo*. Yet it is suggested in Progorelov's 'Warning' that the gentry may have been purged
by the experiences of the last two decades, and Progorelov (speaking
with the distinct accent of Saltykov) implies that a period of regeneration
may be taking place. He, Progorelov, for instance, is clear-sighted
enough to acknowledge the justice of his status as a *propashchii chelovek*,
and he looks forward to the possibility of one day becoming a 'decent
has-been' (*poryadochnyi propashchii chelovek*), a man of duty, goodness,
honour, and industry. Or, if he is himself too decayed to become a
useful member of society, perhaps his offspring will have the chance of
being 'a man in general and a son of his country in particular'.[27] This,
coming at the end of the work, enlarges on a proposition made in the
opening chapter: there, Saltykov expresses the view that though the
present *kul'turnyi chelovek* holds back from social involvement because
he fears the disapproval of the authorities, future generations will have
freed themselves from that fear and take on their social responsibilities.[28]

Saltykov, then, voices and implies some hope for the future, though
on the evidence of the book a better future is only a distant prospect.
Still, there are in *Ubezhishche Monrepo* notes of affirmation, and if they
are not dominant, this is no more than typical of their place in Saltykov's
work as a whole. In general, *Ubezhishche Monrepo* offers proportionately
more than most in the way of evidence for the positive ideals and
opinions of its author. Whether or not they are convincing is another
matter—they did not, for instance, convince Marx, who read and
annotated *Ubezhishche Monrepo* and considered the social and historical
hopes expressed at the end 'feeble and unfortunate'.[29]

[27] Ibid. 398.   [28] Ibid. 283.

[29] See Karl Marks, 'Zamechaniya i pometki na knige M. E. Saltykova-Shchedrina *Ubezhishche Monrepo*', *Druzhba narodov*, 1958, No. 5, p. 26: 'La dernière partie de la Predosterezhenie est très faible; généralement l'auteur n'est pas fort heureux dans ses conclusions
"positives".' For an assessment of Marx's judgement of *Ubezhishche Monrepo* and for lucid and

In composition and style *Ubezhishche Monrepo* is well representative of Saltykov's basic manner of writing. His two chief modes are the reflective and the narrative—the essay and the sketch. Sometimes they are separate, sometimes they overlap. This alternation we find in *Ubezhishche Monrepo*, with the central three chapters providing a narrative core between the reflective first and last chapters. The work benefits from the presence of a narrator-figure throughout, who saves it from the obscurity and turgidity which pose such a formidable obstacle to the would-be reader of many of his other works. It is a feature of *Ubezhishche Monrepo* that the reflective passages, which include the ironic self-revelations of the narrator and the emotional pleas of Progorelov, are little less lively and interesting than the narrative sections.

Irony is a basic tool of the satirist, and Saltykov was one of the supreme ironists in Russian literature. Irony might be defined as the creation of an appearance to draw attention to a—usually critically viewed—reality. This is achieved by various devices of oblique statement and distortion, which act as signals to the reader: for instance, blatant misnomers, exaggeration, and understatement, which any reasonable person will recognize as not in accordance with known or probable fact. 'Distortion' is not a bad general term for the various linguistic and stylistic weapons which constitute the satirist's armoury. Linguistic registers are clearly very important: the inappropriate use of language—the misapplication of elevated or banal words and phrases, the juxtaposition of expressions of different levels—these are common ways by which the writer gives a satirical intonation to his text.

Such devices are fully exploited in *Ubezhishche Monrepo*. The *kul'-turnyi chelovek* narrator's presentation of himself is consistently ironic; he acts the role of unaware self-confessor, revealing his weakness and the faults of Russian society by making propositions that are clearly unacceptable to reason—for instance, his implication that dying or doing nothing might conceivably be forbidden by the authorities, or his uncritical description of how he cheered the monstrous speech about spying made by Gratsianov to the policemen. Gratsianov also acts as the unaware self-confessor. He describes the meetings of police officers held to discuss theoretical questions of peace-keeping, and the debate they had had on the meaning of the official phrase 'with all expedition and rigour' (*s skorost'yu i strogost'yu*)—which, after much deliberation, they interpreted as 'at once and unflinchingly' (*nemedlenno i ne poslablyayuchi*). There is the irony of opposite meaning in his

helpful comment on the work itself, see M. Rev, 'Marks i Shchedrin: nekotorye problemy, svyazannye s izucheniem zamechanii i pometok Karla Marksa na knige M. E. Saltykova-Shchedrina *Ubezhishche Monrepo*', *Acta Litteraria Academiae Scientiarum Hungaricae*, viii (1966), 255–61.

declaration that the modern police keep to the spirit rather than the letter of the law. The normal implication would be of a more liberal approach to cases, but here Gratsianov is speaking in the context of a system which takes repressive measures not only against actions, but also against ideas and opinions: in this situation it is *less* liberal. Similarly, when he calls for 'more freedom, more air', it is more freedom for the police that he is demanding, who will use it to curb the more effectively the liberty of society.

Irony is continually present in the language. We find the use of elevated synonyms: the authorities referred to Church Slavonically as 'the watchmen' (*nakhodyashchiesya na strazhe*); phrases borrowed from official sources and right-wing publicists: N's day-dream of a happy Russia is hastily dismissed as 'the stirring of destructive passions' (*vozbuzhdenie pagubnykh strastei*), the remark that activities to help the peasants 'outside the law' (i.e. the activities of *narodnik* activists) are shrouded by a curtain, to lift which might cause 'something to be shaken' (echoing the official phrase about political agitation, which 'shakes the cornerstones' of society), and so on. These are all part of Saltykov's aesopic stock-in-trade—the familiar system of alternative words, catch-phrases, and circumlocutory images, which are also a kind of 'distortion'. There are the blank references to 'iron rods' (by which you might be ruled), 'ram's-horns' (into which you might be bent), 'fertile places' (in Siberia, to which you might be exiled). Liberal reformist ideas promoted by N in the past are 'philanthropies' (*filantropii*).[30] The real term for official objects is almost always avoided: Gratsianov promises N that his life will not be 'suddenly interrupted' (i.e. by his being arrested), and N refers with marvellous restraint to the police spy planted in his house merely as a 'free-lancing stranger' (*vol'nopraktikuyushchii neznakomets*).

There are other distortions. Seeming incongruities are juxtaposed: 'money-lenders, railway builders, bankers, and *other peculators*'—the logical connection is deliberately distorted to make the critical connection clear; inappropriately grandiloquent epithets and similes highlight the presumptions of those described—the 'newly manifested (*novoyavlennyi*, normally of saints) Russian bourgeois', and the police who 'like unto gods' (*yako bogi*) have the power to read men's hearts. There is also the device one might call the 'literal extension of image' (used by Saltykov more often for humorous than satiric purpose). N, before the arrival of Gratsianov, believes that 'the cup of disasters has been drained', when suddenly he discovers the existence of 'another

---

[30] In a letter of 27 March 1879 to A. N. Engel'gardt Saltykov explained that the word he had originally used here was *propagandy*, but since this had been disallowed by the censors he had been forced to find a substitute. *Filantropii* he considered much better—an interesting, if rare, case of an author's work benefiting from censorial interference. See *SS*, xix(1), 101.

whole tubful' (*chasha bedstvii uzhe vypita do dna . . . i vdrug net! imeetsya nagotove i eshche tselyi ushat!*). Later, N pictures to himself Gratsianov reading his heart—finishing one page, licking his finger to turn over, and so reading on to the end; or he sees himself fleeing from Gratsianov 'as a free bird', 'as a wild steppe horse', 'as a fierce buffalo' (all conventional images), but at the same time acknowledges that Gratsianov is a man who would devour a canary, lasso and break in a wild horse, and convert a buffalo into beef-steaks.

Contrast and paradox are also, of course, related to the 'distortion as indicator' technique, though here the difference is clearly stated and not left to inference. Take one of the climaxes of Progorelov's 'Warning', when he reflects on the present upholders of the principles of 'property, family, and state':

Woe to that city where the street and tavern whine about the sanctity of property; verily in that city some unprecedented robbery is about to happen!
Woe to that place where the publicists cry out . . . that the family is sacred; verily in a little while that place will be the scene of adultery on the most colossal scale! . . .

and so on.[31]

Irony here gives way to what is virtually raillery and abuse. It is part of the blatantly rhetorical weaponry to which Saltykov has frequent recourse. It is not always handled as crassly as here, nor is it always used to negative purpose. Saltykov showed considerable skill at descriptive and 'mood' writing, and if we study the more intentionally soulful passages in his works we usually find them based on fairly elementary rules of rhetoric. Take, for example, the reflective-descriptive passage in which the *kul'turnyi chelovek* records how he passes the time in solitary day-dreaming:

And so I dreamt. Dreamt and felt myself dying, naturally, unashamedly dying. For the first time in my life I savoured the knowledge that nothing would disturb me dying at my leisure, that no one would call me to question or remind me of obligations, that not a single soul would ask of me advice or help, that I had no place to hurry to in order to talk or to do anything, that no organ of the press would shower me with abuse. In short, that I was forgotten, completely forgotten.
Inside the house there was emptiness, silence, and solitude. Outside the house—the same solitude, the same emptiness. Occasionally the park was obscured, as if with a curtain, by falling flakes of snow; occasionally the trees seemed to cast off the yoke of their rigid stillness and, shaken by the wind, they quickened and stirred; occasionally even an ominous moaning sounded in the wood. But my eyes and ears were soon accustomed to these sights and to these sounds.[32]

[31] *SS*, xiii, 387–8.
[32] Ibid. 341.

The devices are obvious—repetition, augmentation, inversion, parallelism, and so on. It is basic, simple, and undoubtedly effective in creating the required atmosphere of negative, isolated living (any number of such passages creating the same effect can be found in *Gospoda Golovlevy*).

There is no space for a detailed examination of the style of *Ubezhishche Monrepo*. In general, though, it can be fairly claimed that it demonstrates well—and better than some of the more complex and diffuse works—the range of Saltykov's skills as a satirist and as a descriptive writer. The absence of one important element should perhaps be noted, and that is the element of the fantastic, which is so strikingly effective in, say, *Istoriya odnogo goroda* or the *Skazki*. Dealing with a 'real' situation, presented by a 'real' narrator, *Ubezhishche Monrepo* offers little scope for fantasy. Even so, it makes a token appearance: the narrator, in describing his agricultural failures, mentions the one cow of his herd which proved to be not barren; as a reward for producing a calf she was given—a year's subscription to *Domashnyaya beseda* (a weekly conservative paper), after which she never produced again! Although an insignificant and isolated example, it is at least a reminder of this characteristic feature of Saltykov's satirical method.

In view of all that has been mentioned—*Ubezhishche Monrepo*'s coverage of the main themes of Saltykov's works, its relevance to the situation of the day, its portrayal of a negative reality and statement of a positive ideal, and its satiric method—the claim for its quintessentialness seems to me reasonable. That, of course, does not make it Saltykov's best work. *Istoriya odnogo goroda*, *Gospoda Golovlevy*, and the *Skazki* undoubtedly excel it in satiric brilliance, emotional power, and versatility. But in their different ways each of these says less, and each is in form exceptional for Saltykov. *Ubezhishche Monrepo* is much more representative of his standard product, the sketch-cycle, distinct though it is among this larger group of works by its coherence, compactness, and near novelistic form. These last qualities make it one of the most readable and accessible of his works. It cannot claim priority over the three best known, but it makes a convenient and instructive fourth in the basic list of Saltykov reading, and as such I would commend it.

Konstantin Bal'mont in Oxford in 1897

By A. G. CROSS

OXFORD's 'Russian connection' is of long standing and distinguished pedigree. Even if none of the four students Boris Godunov sent to England managed to study at the University as was intended, Peter the Great's less than successful attempt at an incognito visit at the very end of the same century initiated a stream of Russian scholars, students, and visitors that has continued through both troubled and peaceful times up to the present. It was in the eighteenth century, in the early years of Catherine II's reign, that the first Russian students earned degrees at Oxford and a Russian ambassador became the first honorary graduand; if the former represented an experiment that was not to be repeated, the latter was the beginning of what may now be regarded as a tradition. More than thirty honorary doctorates have been awarded to Russians at irregular intervals over some two hundred years and the recipients have included a small and distinguished number of creative writers (Vasily Zhukovsky, Ivan Turgenev—exactly one hundred years ago, Korney Chukovsky, and Anna Akhmatova) and literary scholars (M. Rostovtsev in 1919 and, more recently, M. P. Alekseev, V. M. Zhirmunsky, and D. S. Likhachev).[1] Naturally, Oxford does not bestow its degrees lightly and many are the Russians, eminent in their various fields, who have visited and lectured at the University and who have not been honoured. One of the most notable of them in the world of literature was the poet Konstantin Dmitrievich Bal'mont (1867–1942), who visited Oxford on several occasions at the turn of the century.

In 1897 Bal'mont was hardly at the height of his fame but his star was certainly in the ascendant. He had made his literary début over a decade earlier with three unnoticed poems in a St. Petersburg journal, but it was his two collections of verse, *Pod severnym nebom* (1894) and *V bezbrezhnosti* (1895), coinciding with the publications of other poets already dubbed 'Symbolists', which brought him to the attention of the public and led, according to Valery Bryusov, to the creation of an instant 'Bal'mont school' of imitators and admirers.[2] The year 1895 had also seen the publication of two collections of his translations from Edgar Allan Poe, *Ballady i fantazii* and *Tainstvennye rasskazy*, and he was

---

[1] See J. S. G. Simmons, 'Turgenev and Oxford', *Oxoniensia*, xxxi (1966), 146–51. For Russians in eighteenth-century Oxford, see my *'By the Banks of the Thames': Russians in Eighteenth-century Britain* (Newtonville, Mass., 1979), ch. IV.

[2] *Pis'ma V. Ya. Bryusova k P. P. Pertsovu* (M., 1927), 78, quoted in V. Orlov's introduction to K. D. Bal'mont, *Stikhotvoreniya* (L., 1969), 12, n. 1.

then already at mid-point in his version of Shelley's works (*Sochineniya Shelli*, 7 vyp. (M., 1893–9)). In September of the following year Bal'mont married for a second time, and immediately left with his bride for an extended honeymoon tour that was to take them to France, Spain, Holland, Italy—and Oxford. A visit to Oxford was not part of the Bal'monts' original itinerary but during their stay in Paris Bal'mont received an invitation to lecture at the University, which he accepted without hesitation.

The invitation came from William Richard Morfill (1834–1909), with whose name the true beginnings of Slavonic studies at Oxford are rightly and closely associated.[3] Morfill, appointed to a Readership in Russian and Slavonic in 1889, became a Professor in 1900 and worked tirelessly until his death to promote an interest in his subject both at Oxford and further afield. He was the author of some nineteen books, including grammars of five Slavonic languages and histories of Poland and Russia, and he wrote constantly for reviews and journals about Slavonic subjects, particularly literature. Nevertheless, he frequently complained to his friends and correspondents (who included in Russia such well-known scholars as A. N. Veselovsky, A. N. Pypin, N. S. Tikhonravov, P. D. Boborykin, P. I. Veinberg, and K. Ya. Grot, the author of a long and sympathetic obituary of Morfill)[4] about the ignorance and indifference in England towards Russian literature in particular. It is therefore not surprising that when a mutual friend, Prince Vladimir Nikolaevich Argutinsky-Dolgorukov, who was studying at Oxford in 1897, told him about Bal'mont, his poetry, and his translations from Shelley, Morfill welcomed the opportunity to let an Oxford audience hear a contemporary Russian poet discussing the development of his native literature.

Money from the Ilchester Bequest (1866) financed Bal'mont's visit and he joined a line of distinguished Ilchester Lecturers, begun by Morfill himself in 1870. On 30 April the *Oxford University Gazette* announced that 'a Course of four Lectures will be delivered in the French language during the ensuing Term, at the Taylor Institution, by Mr Constantine Balmont, of Moscow, on Contemporary Russian Poetry', and they were duly given in the space of a week on 4, 7, 9, and 11 June at 5.30 p.m.[5] The *Gazette* also provides the title of the first and last lectures—'Russian Poetry in its relation to English. The Founders

---

[3] On Morfill, see James A. H. Murray, 'William Richard Morfill 1834–1909', *Proceedings of the British Academy*, iv (1909), 1–7; J. S. G. Simmons, 'Slavica Tayloriana Oxoniensia', *Cahiers du monde russe et soviétique*, x (1969), 536–45.

[4] Letters from Morfill to the first five scholars as well as to A. F. Onegin, who was then living in Paris, are to be found in the Institute of Russian Literature, Academy of Sciences of the USSR, Leningrad: *Fond* 29, *op*. 1, *ed. khr.* 155; *Fond* 45, *op*. 3, *ed. khr.* 545; *Fond* 93, *op*. 3, no. 856; *Fond* 217, 29011/ccvii bv; *Fond* 250, *op*. 5, no. 158. Grot's obituary of Morfill is in *Zhurnal Ministerstva narodnogo prosveshcheniya*, NS xxvii (May 1910), 35–50.

[5] *Oxford University Gazette*, xxvii (30 April 1897), 437; (25 May), 521.

of the Modern School: Zhukovski, Pushkin, and Lermontov' and 'The Group of young poets—Minski the pessimist: Merezhkovski. Influence of Italian Painting and the English Preraphaelites. Conclusion'.[6] Bal'mont's lectures were never published, but the manuscript is preserved, according to his wife's memoirs, in the Literary Museum in Moscow (TsGALI). However, an interesting review with copious extracts from the first lecture appeared in *Severnyi vestnik* in August 1897.[7] Bal'mont compared the work of Pushkin and Lermontov with that of Tyutchev and Fet, whose influence on the modern generation of poets he was subsequently to emphasize. He also spoke briefly of Maikov, Polonsky, Aleksey Tolstoy, Apukhtin, and other poets. The Russian reviewer reveals that the second and third lectures were in fact devoted to a close analysis of the work of Tyutchev and Fet, whilst the fourth was 'an attempt to characterize contemporary Russian poetry on the basis of the work of a few of its representatives, an attempt that suffers from one-sidedness and exaggerations but is not devoid of originality'.[8] According to the review, Bal'mont's lectures were attended by 'a large audience, highly sympathetic both to the young Russian poet and to the subject of his lectures'.[9] His wife gives a somewhat different version: Bal'mont was disappointed both with the size of his audience, consisting entirely of dons and ladies (for students had more pressing demands on their time), and with the lack of response and real interest. Nevertheless, he evidently enjoyed his stay, working in the Bodleian Library and meeting a number of eminent scholars. Among the latter were several close friends of Morfill, including John Rhŷs (1840–1915), since 1877 the University's first Professor of Celtic and since 1895 Principal of Jesus College, Edward Burnett Tylor (1832–1917), likewise the first Professor of Anthropology (since 1896), Frederick Conybeare (1856–1924), the Armenian scholar, whose researches were to take him to Moscow, and the family of the late Professor Edward Augustus Freeman (1823–92), a Corresponding Member of the Russian Academy of Sciences, author of the monumental *History of the Norman Conquest* (1867–79) and noted for his thesis of 'the unity of history'. Bal'mont with his veritable thirst for languages and his interest in all fields of knowledge and inquiry would have found much to discuss and debate.[10]

---

[6] *Oxford University Gazette*, xxvii (1 June), 539; (9 June), 567.

[7] 'Iz zhizni i literatury', *Severnyi vestnik*, No. 8 (August 1897), 117–22. I am grateful to Mr D. L. L. Howells of the Taylor Institution Library for bringing this article to my attention and for other assistance in the preparation of this study.

[8] Ibid. 122.

[9] Ibid. 117.

[10] Rhŷs and Tylor are named by Orlov (Bal'mont (n. 2), 27) who, however, confused Tylor with Taylor and assumed that he was both head and founder of the Taylor Institution. Conybeare and Freeman are mentioned in the memoir printed below. The careers of all four scholars are outlined in *DNB*.

The Bal'monts left Oxford in the middle of June en route for Italy, missing by a few days Oxford's celebration of Queen Victoria's Diamond Jubilee on 22 June, but having witnessed the visit of H.R.H. the Prince of Wales on 12 May to open the new Town Hall as well as the rowdy weekly Sunday meetings of the local Socialists, unfailingly disrupted by junior members of the University. Before they left, Morfill, a contributor of long standing to *The Athenaeum*, enlisted Bal'mont to provide the annual review of Russian literature and scholarship for that journal. Bal'mont's contributions were to appear for three consecutive years from 1898 before giving way to similar surveys by Bryusov.[11] Back in Russia by the autumn of 1897, Bal'mont busied himself with the publication of a new collection of poetry. *Tishina* appeared the following year and included a cycle of poems entitled 'Iz Anglii': one of them, 'Vecher', dated 'Spring 1897, Oxford', was dedicated to Morfill; another, 'V Oksforde', contained a final third stanza as follows:

Дышат деревья, их пышность нетленна,
Грезят колледжи о Средних Веках.
Зимние думы промчатся мгновенно,
Воды проснутся в родных берегах.
Время проходит, мечта неизменна,
Наше грядущее в наших руках.[12]

But England and Oxford were not to become merely the stuff of dreams and memory. The succeeding years were years of ceaseless travel for the Bal'monts, punctuated by short return visits to Russia to supervise the publication of further collections such as *Goryashchie zdaniya* in 1899 and *Budem kak solntse* in 1901, works which established Bal'mont as Russia's leading, and certainly most fashionable, poet. Bal'mont himself was back in Oxford in July 1900, when Morfill informed K. Ya. Grot: 'We have with us in Oxford P. Vinogradov from Moscow and also K. Bal'mont. The latter has translated very successfully in my opinion the poems of the English poet Shelley. He is now much occupied with the study of old English drama.'[13] He was to pay no less than three further short visits to the University to see Morfill in 1902–3. Possibly 1903 was the year of their last meeting, although Bal'mont was certainly in England, if not in Oxford, on two more occasions before Morfill's death in 1909.[14] Nevertheless, right up to

---

[11] *Athenaeum*, No. 3688 (2 July 1898), 25–6; No. 3740 (1 July 1899), 25–7; No. 3793 (7 July 1900), 23–5.

[12] Bal'mont (n. 2), 134–5.

[13] Grot (n. 4), 48 (Original in Russian). Pavel Gavrilovich Vinogradov (Sir Paul Vinogradoff, 1854–1925) resigned his professorship at Moscow University in 1901 and came to Oxford, where he received an honorary DCL in 1902 and was elected to the Corpus Chair of Jurisprudence in 1903. He was knighted in 1917.

[14] In 1909 Bal'mont wrote an autobiographical sketch entitled 'Liverpul'', which was

that time Bal'mont sent copies of his various works and translations which found their way into the Oxford professor's rich and ever growing library and which bore inscriptions testifying to the Russian poet's high esteem for his friend. Thus for instance he wrote on the title page of *Zlye chary* (1906): 'Poetu i uchenomu, s vechno-yunoi dushoi, Vil'yamu R. Morfilyu. K. Bal'mont. "That Light whose Smile kindles the Universe, / That Beauty in which all things work and move . . ." Adonais. Parizh. 1907. Vesna', and on the third volume of his complete translation of Shelley's works (1907): 'Moemu starshemu bratu, Angliiskomu uchenomu i poetu, tsenitelyu Slavyan, Vil'yamu R. Morfilyu, govorit' s kotorym vsegda takzhe radostno, kak gulyat' v Oksfordskom parke, s chuvstvom uvazheniya i lyubvi, K. Bal'mont. Soulac-sur-Mer, 1907, Leto, Villa Ave Maria'.[15]

Bal'mont became very involved with the revolutionary movement, made common cause with Gor'ky, and alienated many of his former Symbolist friends, especially Bryusov. His anti-government verse made his position in Russia precarious, and at the very end of 1906 he and his wife left again for Paris. He was not to see Russia again until 1913 when a general amnesty was declared to mark three hundred years of the House of Romanov, and Bal'mont returned to a rapturous welcome. He himself was to welcome equally rapturously the 1917 Revolution, but predictably the following years proved difficult and in 1920 he left for Paris with his third wife (E. K. Tsvetkovskaya), never to return to Russia. He died in occupied Paris on Christmas Eve 1942, an old, impoverished, and forgotten man.

It was Bal'mont's second wife, Ekaterina Alekseevna Andreeva (1867–1950), who provides us with a fascinating account of Bal'mont's life from his childhood up to the time of his emigration. Andreeva, a merchant's daughter, worked as a translator and met Bal'mont in 1893. He was then writing poems for his collection *Pod severnym nebom*, which appeared early the following year and duly contained a poem dedicated to her. It was only subsequent to their marriage that Bal'mont travelled outside Russia and it is as a record of their life together at this period that Andreeva's memoirs are unique. She began to write her memoirs only after Bal'mont's death when she herself was in her seventies: they have never been published and are now housed in the Manuscript Department of the Lenin Library in Moscow, where I was allowed to see them and copy the section devoted to the Bal'monts'

concerned, however, not with the English town but with a Russian hotel of that name which Bal'mont had known as a boy. Nevertheless, in the opening paragraph he refers to his visits to England and mentions (in addition to Oxford) Cambridge, London, Warwick, and Stratford-upon-Avon as places he had seen.

[15] I am grateful to the Curators of the Taylor Institution and to the Queen's College, Oxford, for permission to reproduce two of these inscriptions from books which are now part of the Morfill Collection and housed in the Slavonic section of the Taylor Institution Library.

visit to Oxford in 1897. The total manuscript (*Fond* 374, Bal'mont, *karton* 1, *ed. khr.* 52) runs to eighty-seven pages and contains two variants of the Oxford episode, both typewritten, which indicates the attention and importance the author herself attached to it. The first version, according to the over-all pagination, occupies ff. 51–62, with hand-written additions on ff. 50 and 53, and the second, ff. 63–73. The second version or copy contains certain corrections in spelling and grammar which are lacking in the first and these have been incorporated into the version printed here.

Apart from the obvious importance of certain details relating to Bal'mont's activities and to the people whom he met, the interest and charm of his wife's memoirs lie in the evocation of Oxford at the end of the nineteenth century, of an Oxford that has passed but in so many ways still survives, described with both humour and perception and seen unusually through Russian eyes. It seems wholly appropriate that such a description should be published for the first time in *Oxford Slavonic Papers*.

* * *

Весной этого года 1897-го Бальмонта пригласили в Оксфорд читать лекции о русской поэзии. Это устроилось через нашего знакомого кн. Владимира Николаевича Аргутинского-Долгорукова. Молодой человек этот готовился стать дипломатом и жил в Оксфорде для совершенствования в английском языке. Он рассказывал проф. Морфилю (специалисту по славянским наречиям) о переводах Бальмонтом Шелли. Морфиль заинтересовался и пригласил Бальмонта, от имени Тайлоровского Института прочесть серию лекций о русской лирике.

Бальмонт охотно согласился. Он был счастлив поехать на родину его обожаемых поэтов. Он тут же в Париже начал готовиться к этим лекциям. История русской лирики от Пушкина до наших дней, до символистов. Четыре лекции.[16] Они состояли главным образом из стихотворных текстов поэтов. Бальмонт написал лекции по-русски и перевел их вместе со мной на французский язык. Он решил читать их по французски, ему это посоветовали люди, хорошо знающие английские нравы: нельзя читать в Англии по английски, если не знать английский язык в совершенстве. Англичане беспощадны к тем, кто хоть немного коверкает их язык. Были случаи, когда слушатели громко высмеивали лектора-иностранца, делавшего ошибки, и срывали его лекцию.

Один наш знакомый французский писатель Понсеврэ согласился поправить наш перевод. Он вернул нам его с немногими пустяшными замечаниями и с кучей комплиментов. Особенно он хвалил стихотворные переводы, которые сделал Бальмонт к стихам Пушкина, Лермонтова, Тютчева, Фета и др.

Лекции состоялись в Оксфорде в мае-июне, в самый разгар весеннего сезона, когда английская публика съезжается на выпускные экзамены

16 'Оригинал этих лекций находится в Литер. Музее' (Author's note).

колледжей, сопровождаемые торжественными празднествами, спектак-
лями, балами и состязаниями всякого рода, футбольными и другими. Но
главные состязания лодочные. Они происходят на широком водном
пространстве, на слиянии двух рек: Темзы и Оксфорда. Ко времени
празднеств по Темзе прибывают пароходы, их много, должно быть 18,
по числу колледжей. Флотилия выстраивается в ряд у берега одного из
самых обширных и величественных парков Оксфорда. Из этого парка к
воде опускается знаменитая 'Аллея гигантов', аллея старых огромных
вязов. Каждый колледж располагает своим пароходом, над ним раз-
вевается красивое знамя колледжа. Студенты украшают свой пароход по
своему вкусу и желанию, приглашают на него свои семьи, друзей,
знакомых, съезжающихся со всех концов Англии.

Вы с утра можете приходить в гости на эти пароходы к своим знакомым
студентам и профессорам. На каждом пароходе до поздней ночи открыт
буфет с закусками, фруктами, сластями, винами и другими напитками,
шоколадом, кофе, лимонадами.

Вечером на палубах зажигают разноцветные фонари, там устраивают
концертные отделения, танцы для молодежи. Эти ярко освещенные
пароходы с крыш пускают феерверки очень красиво на темной глади воды.[17]

Были два для нас очень интересных зрелища. Торжественное заседание
в честь всех студентов, окончивших курс в Оксфордском университете в
этом году. Оно происходило в очень пышной обстановке; в огромном
круглом зале, на возвышении, в высоких креслах, сидели профессора и их
ассистенты в белых париках с длинными локонами (как мы привыкли
видеть на портретах Мольера и других портретах 17 века), облаченные в
черные длинные мантии. У некоторых рукава их мантий свисали до
пола. Эти лица были самые заслуженные. У студентов 1-го курса рукава
коротенькие, только немного спускающиеся с плечей. Профессора
обращались к окончившим курс студентам с приветственными речами
на латинском языке. Но что это было за латынь! Сначала мы с Бальмонтом не поняли на каком языке они говорили. Они произносили латин-
ские слова с английским выговором, делая английские ударения. Сначала
Бальмонт смеялся, потом рассердился на бесцеремонное обращение с
таким чудным певучим языком, как латинский. Мы ушли, не дослушав
их длинных речей. Я не упустила случая попрекнуть Бальмонта: 'вот
твои любимые англичане спокойно коверкают чужой язык, а от ино-
странцев требуют, чтобы они английский знали в совершенстве'.

Другое еще более интересное зрелище было театральное представление
'Сон в летнюю ночь', которое поставила прославленная труппа Шекспи-
ровского театра (в Стратфорде — место рождения Шекспира — был
театр, построенный специально для постановок шекспировских пьес и
его труппа славилась в Англии).

В Оксфорде 'Сон в летнюю ночь' шел в оригинальной обстановке.
В одном из самых старых парков университета на развесистых ветвях
вековых деревьев были укреплены подмостки. Актеры двигались среди
зеленых ветвей и листьев живых деревьев. Освещена была только сцена

---

[17] 'Нам с Бальмонтом эти празднества на пароходах напомнили испанские
"феерии" на святой неделе, Semana Santa' (Author's note).

фонарями, скрытыми в листве. Парк, где сидели мы, зрители, тонул во мраке. Актеры, уходя со сцены, исчезали, будто проваливались, в темноту ночи. Шорох ветра, пробегающего по ветвям, туман, поднявшийся из-за пруда, а позднее закапавший по листьям мелкий дождь (который заставил некоторых из публики раскрыть зонты) придавал странную реальность этому по-истине фантастическому зрелищу.[18]

На лекциях Бальмонта было немного народу (нас поздравляли, что зала не пустая, как это иногда случалось). На первой лекции было больше публики чем на 4й, человек 60. Бальмонту это показалось мизерно мало, т.к. он привык к полной зале в много сот слушателей на своих публичных выступлениях в Москве, Петербурге и в Париже в русской колонии. И впечатления большого эти лекции не произвели; очевидно, английская публика не заинтересовалась русской поэзией. Очень немногие из слушателей знали имена Пушкина, Лермонтова. В подлиннике их читал конечно один пр. Морфиль. Два, три человека знали их во французских и немецких переводах. И никто не знал, даже по имени, Тютчева, Фета, тем более современных символистов. Бальмонта слушали внимательно и любезно благодарили за 'very very interesting report' (оч. оч. интересный доклад). Но потом никто к нему не возвращался в разговоре. [...][19] На лекции приходили все наши знакомые профессора, много дам, но студенты отсутствовали. Они очевидно были поглощены подготовкой к состязаниям, происходящим здесь ежегодно между Оксфордом и Кэмбриджем.

Студенты проводили все дни в университетском парке на берегу реки: одни гребли на лодках, читая, отдыхая; другие фехтовали, играли в футбол, и этих последних студентов мы часто видели с окровавленными лицами, с поврежденными членами. Мы с Бальмонтом тоже гуляли и часами сидели в этом чудесном парке и наблюдали за нравами английской молодежи. Я долго не могла привыкнуть к виду этих голых молодых людей. Наша русская учащаяся молодежь ходила в то время в мундирах с высокими воротниками, летом в кителях, застегнутых на все пуговицы. Вышитая рубашка с поясом на студенте считалась вольностью, или отсутствие жилета под летним пиджаком. Девушки тоже, даже летом, носили высокие воротники до ушей, длинные юбки. Шея и руки оголялись только на балу.

А тут эти английские молодые люди купались в реке на глазах у всех. Завидя знакомых дам или барышень, они выскакивали из воды, подходили к ним и, отряхнувшись, в одних плавках, мокрые, ходили с ними по парку, непринужденно болтая. Бальмонту они нравились. Правда, они все были красивые, здоровые, упитанные. Бальмонт любовался их сложением, мускулами, их спокойными уверенными движениями. 'Совсем греческие боги', говорил он.

Мы не могли надивиться на жизнь этих юношей. До чего она была

---

[18] 'Mr. Ben Greet's company of woodland players will give performances in Worcester College Gardens on Friday of the fairy scene of "A Midsummer Night's Dream" and on Saturday of scenes from "The Tempest"' (*Jackson's Oxford Journal*, No. 7256 (19 June 1897), 8).

[19] Several lines on the minor French *littérateur* Pontsevrez's quite different reaction to Bal'mont's lectures are omitted here.

непохожа на жизнь наших студентов. Каждый английский студент занимал в колледже, где он учился, 2, 3 отдельных комнаты. У каждого была своя столовая, где он пил чай со своими гостями, своя библиотека, несмотря на то, что при каждом колледже была общая столовая и общая библиотека. Приезжая в Оксфорд учиться, студенты привозили с собой свою прислугу, боя чаще всего, лодку, лошадь, велосипед и т. д.

Почти никто из студентов не ходил на лекции, хотя лекции и в весенний сезон читали до экзаменов. У студентов были 'тюторы',[20] которые подготовляли их к экзаменам.

Я не представляю себе когда они учились. Может быть зимой? Но с 1-го мая они весь день проводили на воздухе, тренировались . . . К 5-ти часам они переодевались, или, лучше сказать, одевались, так как с утра они ходили полуголые, надевали фланелевые светлые костюмы и отправлялись на garden party, где с дамами и девицами играли в теннис, крикет и пр., или уезжали на велосипедах за город, на пикники. К 8-ми они облекались во фраки, обедали у себя в колледже, а после обеда бесконечно долго сидели, курили и пили вино. На эти обеды приглашали гостей. Бальмонт был в нескольких колледжах на таких студенческих обедах и находил их очень скучными. Хозяева были чрезвычайно любезны, гостеприимны, но беседа была принужденная, неинтересная большей частью.

По воскресеньям утром все студенты, с молитвенниками в руках, шли в церковь, где благоговейно присутствовали при совершении мессы.

Бальмонт вспоминал свое студенческое время.[21] Он жил на 25 р. в месяц, которые получал из дому. Другие студенты, его товарищи, считали его богачем, т.к. он обедал каждый день в студенческой столовой (25 к. обед), и у него была теплая комната в меблированных комнатах за 15 р. в месяц с двумя самоварами в день. А как голодали его товарищи! Как они работали чтобы жить и учиться в столицах! Когда плата в русских университетах с 40 р. в год повысилась до 100 р. — это была катастрофа для учащихся, очень много их лишалось высшего образования.

Развлечения и забавы английских студентов тоже были своеобразны и нам мало понятны. Им запрещалось ночью уходить из колледжей. У дверей сидел привратник, наблюдающий, чтобы к ночи все студенты были дома. Колледжи, бывшие монастыри-крепости, были обнесены высокими каменными оградами. Стены их, поросшие мхом, сверху были густо усыпаны битым стеклом, из-под которого торчали железные острия. Перелезть через такую отвесную стену и не сорваться в ров, поросший снаружи колючим кустарником, было трудно и опасно, но может быть именно потому студенты перелезали через такие стены.

Если какой нибудь студент в их общежитии совершал неблаговидный с их точки зрения поступок, 'его хоронили в общественном мнении'. Я видела такие шутовские похороны. Днем, с заженными факелами, студенты, облеченные в траур, с печальными лицами несли черный

[20] 'В роде репетиторов' (Author's note).
[21] In the autumn of 1886 Bal'mont entered the Law Faculty of Moscow University. Within a year he was expelled from the university for his participation in student riots. He re-entered the university in the autumn of 1888 but did not finish the course.

пустой гроб, на крышке которого было написано белой краской имя и фамилия провинившегося. Эта процессия в торжественном молчании обходила весь город.

И еще забава. Каждое воскресенье в Оксфорд приезжали из Лондона социалисты и устраивали митинг на главной площади города. Мы жили рядом с ней на St. John Street и каждое воскресенье невольно присутствовали на этом шумном зрелище. Группа социалистов занимала место в одном углу площади. Собиралась большая толпа горожан. Люди рассеянно слушают речи социалистов, все смотрят на главную улицу, откуда ровно в 5 часов стройными колоннами движутся студенты. Дойдя до площади, они выстраиваются против социалистов. Начинается кошачий концерт: кричат петухами, визжат, свистят, чем то гремят, хлопают, заглушая речи ораторов. Протесты социалистов не помогают. Студенты бросаются на них. Начинается потасовка. Из толпы выходят несколько человек, но немного, и становятся на сторону социалистов. Они дерутся. Толпа остается неподвижным зрителем. Полиция отсутствует. Социалистов окружают и теснят к выходу под рев и гиканье студентов. 'Мы опять придем', кричат социалисты. 'И опять уйдете', кричат студенты. В кольце студентов социалистов выпроваживают из 'нашего Оксфорда', как говорят студенты. Горожане добродушно смеются им вслед и расходятся... до следующего воскресенья.[22]

В Оксфорде студенты англичане держатся обособленно. Иностранцы, учащиеся в их колледжах, не сливаются с ними, как разноплеменная толпа студентов французских университетов. Японцев и негров англичане только терпят в своей среде.

В нашей квартире в Оксфорде жил студент негр, кончавший курс. Он блестяще сдавал экзамены, и его речь, произнесенная им в университетском Парламенте, 'О колониальной политике' была отмечена.[23] Человек он был образованный, говорил на нескольких языках.

Когда Бальмонт нанимал для нас квартиру, хозяйка предупредила его между прочим, что у нее в квартире живет негр. Она сделала паузу и посмотрела на Бальмонта; так как он молчал, она продолжала: 'Очень милый студент колледжа такого-то, и', прибавила она, 'он принц, в его жилах течет царская кровь.' Но это оказалось ее выдумкой. Бальмонт спросил этого негра (Мистера Смита) почему его хозяйка называет 'принцем'. Он, смеясь, ответил, что на расспросы мужа нашей хозяйки, он ему сказал, что он сын вождя известного племени в Африке, и вероятно, этот рассказ и породил в них представление о его царственном происхождении.

Мы хорошо познакомились с этим негром. Он посещал нас, ходил с нами гулять. Мы скоро заметили, что когда он был с нами, наши

[22] Meetings were organized every Sunday by the Oxford branch of the Social Democratic Union. Only occasionally did groups come from London to reinforce the Oxford socialists. One such occasion was Sunday, 5 June 1897, when an undergraduate fired off a revolver. See 'Undergraduates and the Socialists', *Jackson's Oxford Journal*, No. 7522 (22 May 1897), 8, and 'The Socialist Disturbances', ibid. No. 7525 (12 June 1897), 8.
[23] 'В Оскфорде был Парламент для студентов, где они упражнялись в ораторско искусстве' (Author's note).

английские знакомые не так охотно подходили к нам в парке, и никогда не садились в его присутствии на скамью поболтать с нами, как делали это раньше.

Один благожелательный англичанин, приятель Бальмонта, предупредил его очень деликатно, что мне без мужа лучше бы не показываться с негром в общественных местах.

Мы прожили все лето в Оксфорде. Нам там очень нравилось, — и старые монастыри-колледжи с их столетними парками на берегу реки, и окрестности Оксфорда, замки, которые англичане возили нас осматривать.

Утро Бальмонт проводил в знаменитой Бодлеянской библиотеке (лучшей в мире), где читал по ранней английской литературе и поэзии. Здесь он впервые познакомился с поэзией английского мистика Вильяма Блэка, которого стал переводить.[24] Днем он работал у себя.

У нас были три комнаты в небольшом домике. Хозяйка удивлялась, что мы не претендовали на четвертую. 'Где же вы будете принимать гостей?' спросила она. 'В столовой', сказали мы. 'Да, это пожалуй можно, когда вы не будете кушать.'

Бальмонт восхищался порядками английской жизни и самими англичанами. Мне они не нравились, их строго установленные формы общения, банальность их разговоров, их лицемерие. Образчик его мы получили в первый же день нашего приезда в Оксфорд. Приехав из Лондона, мы остановились в одном пансионе, который англичане нам очень хвалили: порядок, тишина, респектабельная хозяйка. Мы прямо с вокзала туда и поехали. Не успели мы осмотреться, как раздался гонг к обеду. Мы спустились в общую столовую. Там уже все пансионеры, человек 6–7, были в сборе. Ждали хозяйку, все стояли и переговаривались полушопотом, как будто в комнате был покойник. Наконец она появилась — старая невзрачная с злющим лицом, осмотрела нас как классная дама, затем, сложив молитвенно руки и воздев глаза к небу, прочла молитву, после чего нас пригласили сесть. Подали нам жидкий невкусный суп, на второе несвежую рыбу, на третье — какую то сладкую кашицу, все это в минимальных порциях. После обеда хозяйка встала и прочла благодарственную молитву ('Это мы благодарим наверно за тухлую рыбу', сказал мне в негодовании Бальмонт. 'Это совсем из Диккенса.'). Тотчас после обеда мы побежали искать себе другое пристанище и нашли отдельные комнаты со столом, где мы были совсем независимы от хозяев.

В первые же дни нашей жизни в Оксфорде мы перезнакомились почти со всеми учеными и профессорами этого университетского городка. Они первые приходили к нам и звали нас к себе, мне приносили от жен пригласительные карточки. Каждый день нас приглашали на завтраки, обеды, garden party и пр., выказывали нам большое внимание. Но знакомясь с нами все без исключения спрашивали нас: 'Are you comfortable

---

[24] A cycle of poems in *Tishina* bore an epigraph from Blake whom Bal'mont came to regard along with Poe as mentors of the Symbolists (see his article 'Praotets sovremennykh simvolistov' in *Gornye vershiny* (M., 1904)). He also translated a number of his poems, including 'Cradle Song' and 'Tyger! Tyger!'.

in Oxford?' (Хорошо ли нам в Оксфорде) и еще: 'не схватили ли мы насморка в такую холодную весну?' И не слушая ответа, ждали, чтобы мы восторгались Англией. Правда, эта весна была исключительно холодная, но англичане это как будто игнорировали. С 1 мая они прекращали топить, и в этот ходод они не топили. В гостиной зажигался камин и дамы декольте, продрогшие в столовой за обедом, грелись у огня. На другой день хозяйка дома делала визиты своим гостям, справляясь, не простудились ли у нее. 'Было бы настолько проще топить', сказала я одной хозяйке дома. 'В мае топить! да что вы, в мае всегда тепло.' Детей вывозили в колясочках в парки, няни все были в белых пикейных платьях и сидели на газонах, трясясь от холода. Но в мае так полагалось.

Они никогда не спрашивали нас о нашей жизни, о России. И обо всем русском говорили свысока, делая одно исключение для Л. Толстого, которому отдавали справедливость: 'О, это большой талант'.

Правда, это при начале знакомства и в светском обществе. Потом они больше открывались, но в большинстве случаев они были самомнительны, надменны, неизменно держались своих старых традиций.

Представляя в обществе Бальмонта, они не говорили, что это русский поэт и переводчик Шелли, а называли его 'мистер Бельмон, профессор при Тайлоровском Институте'. Меня называли 'женой профессора при Тайлоровском Институте Миссис Бельмон'.

В обществе их нельзя было говорить ни о чем, находящемся вне закона.

Бальмонту, заговорившему однажды в обществе о Оскар Уайльде, о его сказках, собеседник не ответил, а потом подчеркнуто переменил разговор.[25]

Старик Морфиль извинялся перед Бальмонтом за то, что на мои расспросы о Мэри Годвин, рассказал о своей встрече с ней во Флоренции, когда она была уже старушкой. О ней, как о незаконной жене Шелли, не полагалось упоминать особенно в обществе дам.[26]

Во всех мелочах жизни у них были ненарушимые правила и обычаи. Попросить у знакомого книгу какого нибудь английского классика считалось неприличным. У каждого человека должны быть свои книги, а если у него их нет, пусть возьмет их в общественной библиотеке. 'Просить книгу Шекспира или Байрона — это также неприлично, как просить у кого нибудь надеть его башмаки или перчатки', сказал один профессор Бальмонту, удивленный видимо, что об этом могут быть два мнения.

Я не могла попасть на бал, дававшийся Оксфордом в музее в честь посещения города королем Эдуардом VII, потому что у меня не было

[25] Bal'mont was a fervent admirer of Wilde. In 1904 he published his translation of *The Ballad of Reading Gaol* and four years later, together with his wife, he translated and published *Salome*. He was also the author of two articles on Wilde: 'Poeziya Oskara Uail'da' (1904) and 'Ob Uail'de' (1906).

[26] The Bal'monts' interest in Mary Wollstonecraft Shelley, née Godwin (1797–1851), author of *Frankenstein* (1818), was predictable. Both Wilde and Mary Shelley are introduced to highlight the hypocritical 'respectability' of English society at this period.

бального платья с достаточно длинным шлейфом, который полагалось иметь в данном случае.[27] Правда, все наши знакомые дамы принимали участие во мне, хотели мне помочь. Одна знакомая предлагала мне свою портниху, другая свое платье даже. Но все шокированно замолчали, когда я придумала нарядиться горничной и сопровождать одну из дам на бал: мне только хотелось взглянуть на убранство музея и танцы в картинной галерее, среди коллекций и картин. Это было единственное, что меня интересовало. Все дамы смутились, а потом засмеялись моей 'шутке'. На другой день эти дамы посетили меня, рассказали о бале, и выражали сожаление, что я не могла на нем быть.

В другой раз в летний жаркий вечер нас пригласила семья Фриман[28] к себе обедать в сад 'запросто'. Бальмонт шутливо спросил: 'Запросто, значит можно не надевать фрака?' 'Как хотите', ответила хозяйка. Бальмонт надел визитку, я летнее платье не декольте. И мы все же почувствовали себя очень неловко, когда увидали хозяек — двух барышень и их тетку декольте, в брилиантах, а мужчин во фраках. 'В чем же состоит ваше запросто?', спросил Бальмонт. 'В том, что мы сидим в саду, сами себе услуживаем, отпустили прислугу, а чай будем пить на траве.' Когда Бальмонт извинился, что мы не en règle, хозяйка перебила его: 'О, иностранцам это простительно', и она сделала вид, что ничего особенного в этом нет. И надо сказать, что этот вечер мы провели очень непринужденно и весело. Барышни качали Бальмонта на качелях, учились у него произносить русские слова, он им читал стихи по-русски. Когда мы собрались уходить, молодежь провожала нас, крича нам вслед по-русски 'досвиданья', 'покойной ночи', 'благодарью', все слова, которые они запомнили.

Бальмонту нравилось все в англичанах — их холодность, внешняя их сдержанность, и он видел в этом их цельность. Он ценил ее, как ценил пылкость, неукротимость и экспансивность испанцев.

Бальмонт сошелся со многими англичанами, посещал их каждый свой приезд в Англию, с некоторыми переписывался долгие годы: с проф. Морфилем, ученым лордом Конибиром, с дочерьми географа Фримана.[29] Кроме того он сотрудничал в английском журнале, посылая ежемесячно туда обзоры русских поэтических произведений, выходящих в России.[30]

Из Оксфорда мы поехали в Виши, где я должна была проделать курс лечения: у меня возобновились припадки желчных колик. Оттуда мы поехали в Италию, на зиму вернулись в Париж.

[27] HRH the Prince of Wales, only later to become King Edward VII, visited Oxford on 12 May 1897 to open the new Town Hall. A detailed description of the Royal visit is found in *Jackson's Oxford Journal*, No. 7521 (15 May 1897), 6–8.

[28] 'Профессор и ученый географ' (Author's note).

[29] I have seen none of these letters. Presumably they are held in TsGALI.

[30] The reference is to *The Athenaeum* (see n. 11).

Characters and Narrative Modes in Marina Tsvetaeva's *Tsar'-Devitsa*

By G. S. SMITH

I

WRITTEN between July and September 1920 and published in two editions in 1922, *Tsar'-Devitsa* is the earliest of Marina Tsvetaeva's longer poems. It belongs to a group of works in which Tsvetaeva made use of thematic and stylistic elements from Russian folk literature. This group includes three other longer poems: *Egorushka*, which was begun in 1920 and left unfinished, *Pereulochki*, and *Molodets*, both written in 1922. *Tsar'-Devitsa* and *Molodets* are of epic proportions; indeed, the 3033 lines of the former make it the longest of all Tsvetaeva's poems. There are no clear parallels to this group of poems in the work of Tsvetaeva's major contemporaries; Mayakovsky was at this time writing poems of comparable length, but neither he nor any other first-rank Russian poet was using Russian folk literature as a principal source. In this respect, Tsvetaeva's work may well have more in common with contemporary trends in Russian music, ballet, and painting than with contemporary trends in literature.

The elements of the plot of *Tsar'-Devitsa*, and the identities and roles of the major characters in the poem, are drawn from the first part of the traditional Russian folk-tale of the same name. Tsvetaeva made no use of the second part of the tale, in which the story is brought to a happy ending.[1] Simon Karlinsky summarizes the plot of Tsvetaeva's *Tsar'-Devitsa* in the following words:

[The poem] tells of the drunken old Tsar, his frail musician-son, and the amorous stepmother (barely hinted at in the Afanas'ev version) who resorts to witchcraft to win the love of her stepson. The heroine of the title is that strange female character recurrent in Russian folklore and epics: the warrior-maiden, a powerful Amazon who usually falls in love with a weak, delicate man. She wins the musician prince by the use of white magic, while the desperate stepmother and her accomplice, the prince's lecherous tutor, fight against the Tsar-Maiden with black arts.[2]

[1] Afanas'ev's collection of Russian folk-tales contains two versions of *Tsar'-Devitsa*. Although differing considerably in detail, they tell the same story, consisting of two parts: (a) The Prince Vasily (or merchant's son Ivan) is betrothed to the Tsar-Maiden; he travels by ship to meet her, but on successive occasions their union is prevented by the Tutor, who, acting on the instructions of the hero's enamoured Stepmother, puts Vasily/Ivan to sleep with a magic needle; (b) Vasily/Ivan, after discovering this treachery, sets out alone and after various adventures makes his way to the Tsar-Maiden in her distant kingdom. See *Narodnye russkie skazki A. N. Afanas'eva* (M., 1957), ii, 227–35 (Nos. 232–3).

[2] S. Karlinsky, *Marina Cvetaeva: Her Life and Art* (Berkeley and Los Angeles, 1966), 223.

This summary is accurate as far as it goes, though whether or in what sense the Tsar-Maiden 'wins' the Prince may be questioned. It does not mention the Wind, which is perhaps Tsvetaeva's most striking addition to the *dramatis personae* of the folk-tale,[3] and it also ignores the important series of events that occurs in the poem after the conclusion of the story of the relationship between the Tsar-Maiden and the Prince.

Tsar'-Devitsa consists of three longer chapters, which Tsvetaeva entitles 'Nights', followed by two much shorter ones, which are entitled 'The Last Night' and 'End'. The three longer chapters contain the story of the three encounters between the Prince and the Tsar-Maiden, and the joint efforts of the Stepmother and Tutor to frustrate their union. These chapters form an elaborately integrated structural unit, held together by the parallel development of the action in each chapter, and the extensive use of literal repetition and minimally contrasting lines. Each of the three chapters is subdivided into two parts, in a proportion roughly of one-third to two-thirds. In each of the three chapters the first part begins at night in the Tsar's palace; the Stepmother attempts to seduce the Prince, with the Tutor taking part as her accomplice. The second part carries the subtitle 'Meeting'; each of the three Meetings opens at early dawn with the Prince awakening and departing in his ship; the Tutor then stabs him with the magic needle, and he sleeps through his ocean encounter with the Tsar-Maiden. On her departure, the Tutor removes the magic needle, and the Prince recovers and recounts his dream recollection of the meeting. In all three chapters, the Tsar-Maiden appears only in the second part, and the Tsar in the first; the Stepmother takes a prominent part in the action in the first part, and makes a final appearance at the beginning of the second part as she covertly observes the Prince's departure.

The last 'Night' and the 'End' deal respectively with the fates of the Stepmother and the Tsar; neither the Prince nor the Tsar-Maiden appear in them as protagonists. In fact, of all the characters that appear in the poem, only the Tsar is present in the last chapter. The last two chapters introduce a considerable amount of fresh material, and their relevance to the remainder of the poem is a serious problem of interpretation. The work would possess a much more clear-cut and symmetrical structure if the last two chapters were removed.

2

Certain qualifications must be made with regard to the use of the term 'character' in discussing *Tsar'-Devitsa*. Clearly, one of the reasons for Tsvetaeva's choice of the folk-tale convention is that it dispenses with

[3] See the commentary of A. Efron and A. Saakyants in Marina Tsvetaeva, *Izbrannye proizvedeniya* (M.–L., 1965), 765–6.

the necessity for verisimilitude in the appearance, actions, and psychology of the protagonists. Thus, no attempt is made in the poem to provide general descriptions of the protagonists' physical appearance; instead, Tsvetaeva invests them with one or two stylized attributes, such as the flaxen hair and cornflower-blue eyes of the Prince, and emphasizes these particular details by repeated reference rather than rounding out the portrait with additional information. The protagonists' movements are not circumscribed by physical laws, and their psychological states are not furnished with any sort of motivation. The focus of interest in the poem, as elsewhere in Tsvetaeva's work, is spiritual rather than physical reality (*bytie* as opposed to *byt*); the characters exist not as studies of credible human beings, but as channels for the exploration and expression of emotional and spiritual states.

The extensive use of parallelism and repetition in the text may suggest that the poem proceeds by the simple accumulation of confrontations between fixed entities, the denouement taking place automatically when the ritual total of three confrontations has been reached. However, this turns out not to be the case with the two principal characters in the poem. One of the most interesting aspects of Tsvetaeva's *Tsar'-Devitsa* is that the Prince and the Tsar-Maiden are not static entities, but instead appear to develop in response to the events of the plot. Tsvetaeva thus departs from the device of abrupt transformation which is characteristic of folklore, and considerably enriches the emotional and psychological range of the original story.

The Prince is the most continually present of the poem's characters. At the outset, he is innocent, refined, and other-worldly. His youth and lack of masculinity are emphasized:

> Не естся яблочко румяно,
> Не пьются женские уста, ... (348)[4]

> Как с конницей-свяжусь-пехотой
> Когда до бабы не охоч! (348)

He is physically frail, and too timid even to 'pick a cornflower in the field'. But after his first meeting with the Tsar-Maiden, the Prince begins to change. He is encountered in the second chapter as he meets his stepmother on the castle battlements (379–82). He disentangles himself from her embrace, but her threat to leap from the battlements into the sea produces the first positive action on his part: he seizes her to prevent her jumping. The Stepmother takes this display of decisiveness and physical strength as a victory for her cause, a sign that she has

[4] Reference will be made throughout to the text of *Tsar'-Devitsa* in the edition cited above (n. 3). Roman numbers in parentheses alongside quotations and in the body of the text refer to the relevant page of this edition.

succeeded in awakening the Prince's sensual instincts. As he prepares
to go out for his second meeting with the Tsar-Maiden, the Prince
himself gives expression to this new sense of his own powers:

> Смородина — кислая,
> А я — молодец!
> Трех быков на вертеле
> Сгублю, не щадя!   (384–5)

The Prince is now much more incisive than at first in his attitude towards the Tutor. He curses him:

> Чтоб весь век не пил-не ел, чтоб зачах!   (387)

And when the Prince is stabbed by the magic needle, he resists the onset
of sleep:

> Но спорит, но всю свою мощь собирает,
> Но пальцами веки себе разрывает . . .   (391)

In the first part of the third 'Night', the Prince revives his father with
his music. Where the old Tsar had previously treated his son with
dismissive contempt, he now expresses approval and even admiration:

> И кудри-то — шапкой!
> Стан — рюмки стройней!
> Вот что бы без баб-то —
> Рожать сыновей!   (401)

The Stepmother's dance, which follows this scene, is an outstanding
example of Tsvetaeva's eroticism. It is significant that the Prince
willingly provides the musical accompaniment to the dance. The
sequence of couplets describing the beginning of the dance shows the
Prince and Stepmother acting in concert as musician and dancer:

> Заиграл сперва гусляр так-от легонечко,
> Ровно капельки шумят по подоконничку.
> Та — рябь рябит,
> Плечьми дрожит. . . .
> Отпустил гусляр своих коней стреноженных —
> Прократилась дрожь волной до быстрых ноженек.
> Как тигр-лежебок
> Готовит прыжок.   (402–3)

This climactic scene culminates in the Tsar's blasphemous baptism of
the couple in wine, his impious marriage pronouncement over them,
and the Stepmother's triumph as at last she takes physical possession of
the Prince (405–8). The Prince submits after the Tsar has threatened
first to bind him forcibly to the Stepmother, and then to smash his

psaltery if he does not kiss her on the lips. The figurative trial of strength between the attraction of the Stepmother on the one side and the Tsar-Maiden on the other is articulated in the three whispered arguments the Prince hears the next evening between the two hairs, the traces of the two women's kisses, and the two tears (409–11). This contest is not resolved in favour of one side or the other. But as he sets forth for his third meeting with the Tsar-Maiden, the Prince has clearly become even less like his original self as a result of spending the previous night in the Stepmother's arms. The change in the Prince is emphasized by a parallel formula. In the first 'Night':

> Слабыми руками
> Вдоль перил витых,
> Слабыми шажками
> С лестничек крутых. (350)

In the second 'Night':

> Смелыми руками —
> Вдоль перил витых,
> Резвыми шажками
> С лестничек крутых. (385)

And in the third 'Night':

> Жаркими руками
> Вдоль перил витых,
> Шалыми скачками
> С лестничек крутых. (411)

From his original starveling state, the Prince has developed into a hero:

> Какой тут заморыш!
> Богатырь, ей-ей! (411)

The cause of the transformation—the loss of innocence through the heat of the Tsar-Maiden's kiss and the honey of the Stepmother's—is made plain:

> Ох, ожог, знать, лютый!
> Не простой, знать, мед! (412)

As the Prince sails to meet the Tsar-Maiden for the third time, he curses the Tutor even more confidently than before. It is now made plain that the Prince has taken over some of the masculine and martial characteristics of the Tsar-Maiden. He is pictured in an heroic posture:

> В сапожке казанском ногу
> На борток поставил он. (420)

This gesture has earlier been allotted to the Tsar-Maiden, in the first 'Night':

> Сапожок чрез борток,
> Ногой легкою — скок . . .   (369)

—and in the second 'Night':

> И — сапожок через борток . . .   (395)

The Prince's glance is likened to a sabre, and he is made to review the clouds, whose power is now literally under his foot (just as the Tsar-Maiden was first seen in the poem in the act of reviewing her troops):

> То не ладан-пар
> От воды встает,
> То войскам — гусляр
> Производит смотр.
>
> Не крестьянским полкам голодным —
> Золотым облакам господним.   (421)

By the time the Prince is struck down for the third time by the magic needle, he has become a figure of power, with the clouds parting obediently before his commanding gesture. His last action in the poem, after he has reviewed—not in dream this time, but written in the clouds —his three encounters with the Tsar-Maiden, is to strike dead his evil opponent, the Tutor; he then dives into the waves 'to obtain his treasure' (428). In the final encounter, the Prince's calling as a musician is played down; he sings and plays to attract the Tsar-Maiden, but his song is a lament in which he bitterly regrets having devoted his life to art instead of practical affairs (419).[5] By the end of his part in the story, then, the character of the Prince has undergone a radical change.

The same is true of the Tsar-Maiden. She is first seen as the virago of the original folk-tale—boisterous, crude, and aggressive. She is made to state her contempt for men and her dedication to martial achievement in argument with her Nurse, the innocent counterpart to the Prince's evil Tutor. She stands alone, needing no kin besides the elements:

> Огнь — отец мне, Вода — матерь,
> Ветер — брат мне, сестра — Буря.
> Мне другой родни не надо!   (352)

---

[5] This song echoes Tsvetaeva's lyric 'Kto doma ne stroil' (1918).

The Tsar-Maiden decides, however, that the Prince would make an ideal partner for her because, since he is so effeminate, he presents no threat to her identity:

> Баб не любишь? Драк не любишь?
> Ну, тебя-то мне и надо!
> Как, к примеру, Дева-Царь я,
> Так, выходит, — Царь-ты-дева!
> Уж с таким-то голосочком
> Муж за прялку не засадит!　　　　　(354)

Her contemptuous treatment of the Tutor at the first meeting anticipates the Prince's eventual attitude towards him; the parallel is reinforced by her reference to him as a spider, which anticipates his transformation into a spider in the third chapter (415). At their first meeting, the Tsar-Maiden treats the sleeping Prince as an infant, almost even as a toy:

> Будет грудь моя стальная
> Колыбелочкой тебе.　　　　　(366)

Her triple christening of the Prince (366–7), however, already contradicts the aims with which she began; for whereas she stated that she needed a passive mate who would not detract from her military might, she now bids the Prince grow in strength until he is more powerful than she:

> Чтоб цельный полк поклал перстом,
> Чтоб первый гром пред ним ползком,
> Чтоб Деву-Царь согнул кольцом —
> Младенчика крещу!　　　　　(366–7)

It seems therefore that the Tsar-Maiden herself predicts and sets in train the Prince's development; the element of connivance in one's own downfall finds a parallel in the Prince's playing for the Step-mother's dance. The Tsar-Maiden also gives the Prince strands of her tough hair to string his psaltery (368), thus strengthening the element of music, to which her own nature is at this stage strongly opposed. At the second meeting, the Tsar-Maiden is shown to have become more sensitive to the Prince's music than even her own 'wonder-sailors' (389–90). Her reaction to the Prince's being asleep at first echoes the condescending amusement she displayed at the first meeting:

> «Агу, агу, младенец!»
> Хохочет, подбоченясь.　　　　　(393)

But then comes the first decisive evidence of change in her: she sheds
tears over the Prince, and identifies them with her pride:

> Кровью на немую льдину . . .
> — Растопись слезой, гордыня,
> Камень-скала!   (394)

—and this is followed by the awakening of self-questioning and doubt
(394).

Paralleling the Stepmother's temptation of the Prince is the Tsar-
Maiden's encounter with the Wind (416–19). The Wind, in response
to the Tsar-Maiden's questions about her beauty and sweetness, reminds
her of her former attributes:

> Ты — наш цвет военный!
> Я — твой неизменный!   (416, 417)

The Tsar-Maiden's renunciation of her former character causes the
Wind first to cajole and then to threaten; the Wind's final appeal is to
the sterility of union with him, recalling the Tsar-Maiden's own
defiant proclamation of self-sufficiency in the first chapter:

> От моей перинки
> Не пойдешь брюхатой!   (418)

But as soon as the Tsar-Maiden hears the Prince's song, the Wind is
contemptuously dismissed:

> Отстранись-ка, Ветер,
> Рваное крыло!   (420)

The Tsar-Maiden's declaration of love for the sleeping Prince at
their third and final meeting is an incantation of extraordinary power,
even in the context of Tsvetaeva's customary emotional extremism.
Her kinship with the elements is now denied:

> Царю не дам,
> Огню не дам,
> Воде не дам,
> Земле не дам.   (423)

She renounces her former assertive pride, which she now blames for
her unhappiness (424); she recognizes the value of passivity:

> Кто спит, — тот пьян, кто спит — тот сыт.
> Да, цветик благовонный!   (424)

And there appears in her the unprecedented feminine quality of tenderness:

> С великой нежностью ему
> Разглаживает шнур-тесьму... (424)

Her final act in the renunciation of her former self is to break her sabre (425); she then tears out her heart and casts it into the sea. The Wind immediately returns to occupy the hole in her breast, and this time is greeted as a brother by the Tsar-Maiden (426). Her fate is explained when, at the end of the dream-memory in which he sees all their three meetings, the Prince reads the message she has traced with her sabre. She has disappeared for ever into oblivion:

> Нигде меня нету.
> В никуда я пропала.
> Никто не догонит.
> Ничто не вернет. (428)

Neither the Prince nor the Tsar-Maiden reappears in the poem after the third 'Night'. The course of their relationship has involved their exchanging certain aspects of their characters: he from feminine passivity to alert aggression, and she from masculine abrasiveness to tender contemplation. It is in this respect that the full extent of the failure of lovers to connect (разминовение), which Tsvetaeva herself identified as the essence of the poem,[6] is revealed. A. Efron and A. Saakyants assert that

The Tsar-Maiden and the Prince in Tsvetaeva's poem personify opposed and incompatible principles: the active—the 'Warrior' (the Tsar-Maiden), and the passive—the 'Angel' (the Prince). The love of the Tsar-Maiden for the Prince is the sun's attraction for the moon, whose meeting is impossible.[7]

The quotation that supports this assertion ('Меж Солнцем и Месяцем / Верста пролегла') is taken from the poem's first 'Night', and does not hold true of the later stages of the relationship between the two characters. The final force of the tragedy, and the full meaning of Tsvetaeva's term разминовение (which is a dynamic rather than a static concept), could be said to stem not from an immutable incompatibility between the two characters concerned, but rather from the effect their relationship has on them: each moves towards the extreme represented by the other, but they fail to find a meeting-point where compatibility and stability would be achieved.

---

[6] Quoted in Tsvetaeva, *Izbrannye proizvedeniya* (n. 3), 765.
[7] Ibid.

3

Around the central relationship in the poem are disposed several secondary ones. Only the Prince and the Tsar-Maiden are evolving characters; the other figures in the poem embody fixed principles.

The Stepmother belongs to what is probably the most numerous category of characters in Tsvetaeva's poetry: the adulterous wife. She is the Tsar-Maiden's chief rival for the Prince, and seems to have won the victory after her dance in the third 'Night'. Her malign influence, exercised through the Tutor, is the cause of the Prince's enchanted sleep during his three meetings with the Tsar-Maiden; she is ultimately disposed of by the Tsar-Maiden's discarded companion, the Wind. She is the object of the Tutor's lust, and gives herself to him twice (347, 384) in repayment for his putting his black powers at her service. He is ultimately killed by the Prince. The Stepmother and the Tutor act in concert as embodiments of the forces of evil. Their essential similarity is emphasized by the repeated use of the colour black in descriptions of them, and by the use of reptile and insect imagery. One of the Tutor's transmogrifications is into a spider, and he is finally crushed like an insect (428); and when the Stepmother is cast from the Wind's back to crash to her death on the rocks below, her spirit crawls away in the form of a serpent (432). The Stepmother and the Tutor, however, are strongly contrasted physically: she is continually described as young and beautiful, he as old and ugly. There is also a significant difference in the way the two characters are presented. The Tutor is unmitigatedly negative; he is sly, cowardly, corrupt, and despised by everyone. His only drive is sexual lust for the Stepmother. Though the Stepmother is also driven by sexual passion, understanding and forgiveness are asked for her at several points in the poem, and there is no parallel in the Prince's attitude to her for the loathing he feels for the Tutor.

The figure of the Wind acts as a counterpart to the Stepmother: the Wind is a rival for the Tsar-Maiden's affections as is the Stepmother for the Prince's, but the Wind is sterile and sexless. Whereas the Stepmother's sensuality is never presented in a negative light, the Wind is prurient and voyeuristic. This aspect of the wind in general is mentioned in several asides (351, 378) before the character of the Wind makes its first appearance in the third 'Night'. At this point (416–18), the Wind's temptation of the Tsar-Maiden parallels the Stepmother's dance at the beginning of the chapter; the Wind is rejected, however, and does not reappear until the very end of the third 'Night' when the Tsar-Maiden tears out her heart. The Wind plays an important part in the last 'Night'; it is conjured by the Stepmother in her lament over the Prince's failure to return (429–30).

The Wind lies to the Stepmother, telling her that the Prince is still alive, but unhappy under the Tsar-Maiden's domination; the Stepmother then mounts the Wind to fly off and destroy the Tsar-Maiden. True to the duplicity it had shown earlier, the Wind then casts the Stepmother to her death, and this is its last contribution to the action of the poem. The figure of the Wind is an original addition by Tsvetaeva to the *dramatis personae* of the original folk-tale. Its most important function in the poem is not the role it plays in the plot, but rather the contrast its affections provide with those of the Stepmother. The Wind articulates a type of affection that is asexual and expresses itself in comradely action by the characters concerned, which contrasts strongly with the heterosexual affection the Stepmother feels for the Prince.

Like the other characters, the Tsar[8] is not depicted in naturalistic terms; in his case, though, the element of caricature is stronger than with anyone else. He is presented as a lord of misrule, the epitome of debauched irresponsibility. He does not appear at all in the first 'Night', though his characteristic theme is foreshadowed in the Tsar-Maiden's instructions to her retinue when she sets out for her first meeting with the Prince:

> Чад не балуйте, баб не бейте,
> Мечом рубите новизну!
> А помянуть меня — пропейте
> Сегодня всю нашу казну! (357)

The Tsar is central to the action in two parts of the poem. He makes his first appearance in the opening scene of the second 'Night', a scene of knock-about slapstick which ends when he brings down his tent about his ears with his drunken staggering (371–4). This scene, however, is keyed into the poem's system of elemental imagery through the Tsar's extended contrasts between the love of others for the ocean and his own for his sea of wine (372–3). The Tsar's dedication to debauchery reaches new heights in the invocation that opens the third 'Night'. His abandonment of responsibility now begins to take on a more ominous colouring, however. He himself invokes the ruin that is eventually to provide the poem's climax:

> Подымайтесь, воры-коршуны-мятежники!
> Для костра свово я сам припас валежнику....
>
> Рухай-рухай, наше царство разваленное! (398)

The Prince then reminds his father that he is his son, and that in the Stepmother he has another dependent; this shocks the Tsar into

---

[8] The two versions of *Tsar'-Devitsa* in Afanas'ev's collection differ with respect to the status of the Prince's father: in one (No. 232) he is a merchant, in the other (No. 233) a tsar.

sobriety and then the swoon from which the Prince's playing revives him. The Prince's art thus provides the first link in the pattern of events that is to lead to the Stepmother's embrace. When the Tsar recovers, his attitude to the Prince has changed; he acknowledges his paternity, but will still not accept the implications (401–2). The Tsar's forcing his wife and son into each other's arms is the most striking example in the poem of a character conniving in his own downfall.

The actual downfall is the subject of the poem's problematical final chapter. Here, the Tsar's own call to rebellion and destruction is answered, and his increasingly desperate protestations, attempted bribery, vain appeals to priests and merchants, are swept aside by the murderous rabble. At the end of the poem, the Tsar is associated with the evil of the Stepmother and Tutor when he is given an insect epithet: Царь-Комарь.

The tonality of the final chapter is strikingly different from that of the remainder of the poem. The folkloristic colouration in lexis, imagery, and versification is retained, but the setting is no longer the fairy-tale world. Instead, the final chapter takes place in the context of a well-defined feudal society, where discontent stems from social injustice, oppression, and material need, rather than from sorcery or elemental affinities. The rabble begins its confrontation with the Tsar with an appeal:

> Царь, залечивай
> Раны-немощи!   (433)

But his outraged rebuke strengthens their desire for retribution, and his protests, which eventually degenerate into pathetic wheedling, are swept aside by the mob's thirst for revenge and destruction:

> — Пощадите мою спинку, голубчики!
> Всем овчинки привезу на тулупчики!
> — Нет, Царь, не до шуб!
> Тебя под тулуп.   (435)

The figure of the Tsar, despite the transition from braggadocio to wheedling at the very end of the poem, remains a caricature, standing for an extreme of self-indulgence and lack of responsibility towards duties and dependents.

The appearance of the mob at the end of the poem adds a new dimension to what has gone before. Where the other characters act alone in pursuing personal ends, the mob defines itself and acts as a collective entity:

> — Ой, Боже, да кто ж вы?
> — А мы — бездорожье,
> Дубленая кожа,

Дрянцо, бессапожье,
Ощебья, отребья,
Бессолье, бесхлебье,
Рвань, ягоды волчьи, —
Да так себе — сволочь!   (434)

They identify themselves in the very last lines of the poem in the following words:

Да, Царь-Кумач,
Мы — Красная Русь!
Твоя мамка мы, кормилка никудашная,
Русь кулашная — калашная — кумашная!
Ша — баш!   (435)

The mob's identification of itself as 'Red Russia' suggests a parallel between the events of the poem and those of Tsvetaeva's own times. However, there is nothing in the preceding events, issues, and tonality that would support such a parallel. The colour red, and also the coarseness and physical violence of the mob, have previously been associated with the Tsar-Maiden in her original state, and the events of the 'End' could possibly be seen as the belated and vicarious triumph of the principle she represents, compensating for the frustration and eventual tragic outcome of her meetings with the Prince. However, the triumph of the mob is not achieved over the elements of sensitivity, passivity, gentleness, and music which in the figure of the Prince originally contrast with the Tsar-Maiden's principle, but over his father, the Tsar. And the Tsar has more in common with the mob than does the Tsar-Maiden: their riotous behaviour and summons to chaos are anticipated by his actions and words. The very last passage of the poem draws attention to this affinity through the epithets 'Царь-Кумач' and 'Русь... кумашная'. It is the absence from the climax of the poem of any equivalent for the values represented by the Prince that is the principal reason for the insufficient integration of the poem's climax with what has gone before.

4

The bulk of the text of *Tsar'-Devitsa* is presented objectively, in several different modes. Chief among these is direct speech by the characters, both monologue and dialogue; much use is made of dialogue with extensive parallelism between the words of the two speakers. Also, songs are interpolated into the text at several points. Passages of direct speech tend to be linked by short sections of text in which action is described without evaluation. However, *Tsar'-Devitsa* is peopled by more than the characters discussed above; there is also a narrator, who emerges in different guises at different points in the text.

In some passages, the narrator addresses the reader directly with an exhortation or warning, e.g.

От бабы Иосиф-то
Нагишом — берегись!
На женском волосике
Не один уж повис! (397)

After the Stepmother's dance and her serpentine embracing of the Prince, the narrator intervenes to direct the reader's moral reaction:

Стар и млад — не суди!
Этот жар — из груди
Должен в грудь перебечь,
Аль всю суть нашу сжечь.

У цыгана — луна,
У буяна — война,
У дворянчиков — честь,
У нас — кровь одна есть.

Кровь, что воет волко́м,
Кровь — свирепый дракон,
Кровь, что кровь с молоком
В кровь целует — силком! (408)

The last five lines of this passage are especially important. The narrator speaks here on behalf of a collective 'we', identifying with the reader. This 'we' does not include all human beings; it excludes in this case the gypsy, the brawler, and the petty gentry. This passage also, by introducing the reptile imagery associated with the stepmother ('свирепый дракон'), correlates her sensual passion with the possessive, fiercely maternal passion of the Tsar-Maiden for the Prince ('кровь с молоком'). The culmination of the collective use of 'we', and the identification of this 'we' as 'народ крещеный' occur in the apocalyptic opening of the final chapter of the poem, which in a sustained architectural image presents an hierarchical system of social relations, and states that this system can be reversed momentarily at the behest of a Fate over which human beings have no control:

Над подвалами — полы,
Над полами — потолки,
Купола — над потолками,
Облака — над куполами.
Там — про наши дела
Пальцем пишет — Судьба.

Пишет — ровно плугом пашет:
Не до грамоты ей нашей!
Берегись, народ крещеный:
Пишет прописью саженной!

Веселись, пока веселый!
Над *подвалами* — престолы.
Как нашлет Бог грозу,
Был вверху, стал внизу.

На́д подвалами — престолы,
По́д подвалами — погосты,
С черной костью нашей рабской,
С мертвой плотью нашей скотской.
Сверху — страсть, снизу — смрад...

А еще рабов винят!   (432)

Besides these instances where the narrator speaks directly to the reader and identifies with him by using the first person plural, there are several examples in the poem of the use of the first person plural by the narrator which refer only to him, in the conventional epic manner:

Песнь прежалостную тут мы споем ...   (358)

И еще-то мы прибавим к сему ...   (358)

Как та песнь сложилась —
Нам-то знать почем?

Не своей охотой —
Дуло у виска!
Не своей работы —
Смертная тоска!   (414–15)

However, at other points in the text the narrator speaks in the first person singular. At the very beginning it is made clear that there is a single female figure directing the narrative:

Соврала, что палочкой:
Перстом светлым, пальчиком.   (341)

This first-person narrator sometimes suggests a sympathetic association with the Prince:

Лежит Царевич мой бессонный ...   (348)

She speaks of the wind in the same way:

Даровой рабочий —
Ветерочек мой!   (378)

And she sighs for a real lover as beautiful as the Prince in her poem:

> Живого такого
> Напеть бы дружка!   (390)

At other points in the poem, the narrator uses the first person plural in order to speak on behalf of women in general; referring to the wind:

> Кто цепь нашу грубую
> Раньше всех расклепал,
> Кто прежде супруга нам
> Шейный плат растрепал.   (378–9)

In this role she comments on feminine jealousy and selfishness:

> Оттого ли бабам в любовный час
> Рот горячий-алый — дороже глаз,
> Всё мы к райским плодам ревнивы,
> А гордячки-то — особливо!   (395)

> На миру монашество —
> Что землю грызть!
> Ну, а бабья наша тут
> Молчать — корысть.   (405)

The female narrator does not argue a feminist case; rather, she is concerned to warn men against women:

> В чудный час передвосходный
> Мой совет тебе — кто б ни был!
> Меняй страстный путь на водный!
> Бросай бабу, — иди к рыбам!   (360)

She identifies masochism as a characteristic female response:

> Бабе: дура! она: ро́дный!
> Ты ей в рыло, она: ми́лый!   (360)

The advice to men to abandon women and take to the ocean is referred to again in the Stepmother's song as the Prince sets out for his second meeting with the Tsar-Maiden; the conclusion is that man's attempt to escape is futile, since woman and the ocean are identical:

> Ведь всё то ж тебя ждет
> И у жен и у вод:
> Грудь — волною встает,
> Волна — грудью встает.

> И опять ни к чему
> Тебе вольный полет!
> Никому не уйти
> Да из женских тенёт!   (386)

The most sustained intervention by the female narrator occurs in the second 'Night'. Here, after an opening scene in which the Tsar is the most prominent character (371–4), the transition to the Stepmother is effected by a scene in which the narrator conducts her reluctant lover secretly to the Stepmother's chamber:

> Так. — Засим, дружок, дай руку.
> Не робей, — плечом не трону!
> Это — детская наука,
> Я китайской обучёна.   (374–5)

The narrator soon identifies herself as the Poet:

> Мы — поющие, — что птицы:
> Разве что перо на память!   (375)

The lover's helping her off with her necklace, and the reference to rustling skirts, anticipate the Stepmother's dance in the next chapter. The narrator refers to the 'kitchen of feminine deception':

> В кухню женского обману
> Поспешай, Самсон с Далилой!
> Здесь из зорь творят румяна,
> Из снегов творят белила...   (376)

There follows the most remarkable example in the poem of explicit toying with the potentialities of first-person narration: the narrator's psychological reality threatens to destroy the fictional reality when the narrator is tempted to abandon her story and lose herself in her lover's kiss:

> (Перед главным, седьмым,
> Прижми губы к моим!)
>
> Сердце к сердцу, устье к устью...
> Окунуться в реки эти —
> Всех Цариц с тобой упустим,
> Всех Царевичей на свете!   (377)

But this temptation is overcome, and the narrator asserts the priority of her role as poet over her role as lover:

> Отпусти! Оторвись!
> Мы рассказывать взялись!   (377)

And the lover is then dismissed with a warning against the dangerous sensual power that is combined with poetic power:

> Коль опять себе накличешь
> Птицу, сходную со мною,
> Знай: лишь перья наши птичьи,
> Сердце знойное, земное...
>
> (Площадной образец,
> Каких много сердец.)
>
> И еще, дружок, запомни:
> Мы народ вдвойне пропащий!
> Так, коли поем красно́ мы, —
> Так еще целуем слаще...   (377)

At no point in the remainder of the poem does the narrator intervene so explicitly or at such length as in this passage.

5

Marina Tsvetaeva's *Tsar'-Devitsa*, then, contains significant departures from its folkloric source in respect of characterization and narrative mode. The effect of introducing development in the main characters and variety in the mode of narration is to increase the work's dynamism and its complexity; the most significant gain is probably the heightened emotional impact that these devices yield. Tsvetaeva does not shrink from explicit attempts to guide the reader's responses, to enrol the reader's participation in the emotional problems that stand at the centre of the poem. However, the devices of characterization and narration are not employed cumulatively or with perceptible aesthetic ordering. The love relationship that is the central theme of the poem reaches its tragic climax well before the end of the work, and the matter that comes after this climax is unsatisfactorily integrated with the main theme. Similarly, the maximally personal appearance of the feminine narrator occurs in a digression approximately one-third of the way through the work, and no further use is made of this device. It is significant that Tsvetaeva never attempted another work of a length comparable with *Tsar'-Devitsa*; *Molodets*, which also uses folk motifs, is shorter by almost 1,000 lines, and its narrative structure and characterization are significantly less complex than are these elements in *Tsar'-Devitsa*. *Tsar'-Devitsa* freely combines elements of the epic, drama, and lyric, but fails to achieve a satisfactory integration of the three; in Tsvetaeva's subsequent work, though purity of genre is not characteristic, there is a significant tendency towards greater homogeneity in this respect than is the case with *Tsar'-Devitsa*.

Oxford Slavonic Papers, I–XIII (1950–1967)

A List of Contents and an Index

By J. S. G. SIMMONS

THE year 1979 sees the eightieth birthday of Sergey Aleksandrovich Konovalov, Professor of Russian at Oxford from 1945 to 1967; it also marks thirty years since the conception of his brain-child, *Oxford Slavonic Papers*. It is, therefore, an appropriate year in which to look back on the thirteen volumes of the journal which appeared under his editorship between 1950 and 1967; and for someone who was his pupil and colleague (and an associate in some of his editorial labours) to provide—as a birthday offering—keys to the volumes in the shape of a list and a general index of their contents.

Editing and publishing have always appealed to Sergey Aleksandrovich. While he was Professor of Russian at Birmingham University (a part-time Chair which he held *in commendam* with his Oxford Lecturership from 1929 to 1945) he was responsible for the publication of bibliographical surveys of research work in Eastern Europe from 1932 to 1934, and for the pioneer *Memoranda* and *Monographs* on Soviet and Polish affairs which appeared between 1931 and 1940. When, as a result of the Scarbrough Commission's recommendations, special grants became available in 1947 for the encouragement of Slavonic studies at Oxford and other British universities, though his first concern was naturally for personnel, the publication of teaching aids (for example, the *Oxford Russian Readers* series) received a high priority. On a less utilitarian plane, since Oxford possessed substantial manuscript and printed library resources in the field, research could be expected to develop. Moreover, there were already within the University (some of them formally outside the Medieval and Modern Languages Faculty) a number of scholars who had made distinguished contributions to Russian studies, and the Ilchester Lectures brought other Slavists from elsewhere in Britain and from abroad into the Oxford orbit. It was in answer to these publication needs, and with the support of a subsidy from Scarbrough funds, that the issue of an annual volume of studies, to be known as *Oxford Slavonic Papers*, was in 1949 proposed to and accepted by the Clarendon Press.

The journal's declared aim was 'the publication of articles, lectures, and documents dealing directly or indirectly with the languages, literatures, and history of Russia, and the other Slavonic countries' and, as its Founder-Editor, Sergey Aleksandrovich showed remarkable enterprise and determination in gaining distinguished contributors for it. At first they were mainly Oxonian—Sir Maurice Bowra, Warden of Wadham, opened the first volume with an essay on Pushkin which he had earlier delivered as an Ilchester Lecture (he followed it two years later with a parallel piece devoted to Lermontov). Another head of a House, the historian B. H. Sumner, Warden of All Souls—also an Ilchester Lecturer—contributed a characteristic interpretation of the theme of Russia and Europe to the 1951 issue, and another All Souls scholar, Isaiah Berlin, published in the same volume the essay on Tolstoy's historical scepticism which was to be widely acclaimed when a revised version of it was published a couple of years later under the less austere title of *The Hedgehog and the Fox*.

The tradition of publishing documents and of giving publicity to manuscript and other rare materials in Oxford libraries began with the first volume of the journal—with the first of Sergey Aleksandrovich's documentary excursions into seventeenth-century Anglo-Russian relations, and with a study of the circumstances surrounding the printing of Ludolf's Russian grammar at Oxford in 1696. Slavonic manuscripts and early printed books in the Bodleian Library were publicized in the second volume, which also included the first articles by non-Oxonian scholars—Nicholas Bachtin of Birmingham University and Pierre Pascal of the Sorbonne, both of whom had delivered their contributions originally as lectures at Oxford. In Volume III the scope of the journal was for the first time extended into the non-Russian Slavonic field with an extensive study of Slavonic metrics developed from his Ilchester Lecture by Roman Jakobson of Harvard University—the journal's first American contributor. (Kiril Taranovski of the University of California was later to touch on a similar theme with a paper on Serbo-Croat metrics which appeared in Volume IX.) The American connection was later further strengthened by, for example, John Hazard of Columbia on Russian law (IV) and by a trio of articles connected with the fortieth anniversary of scholarly activity by George Vernadsky of Yale (V).

The Russo-centrism of *Oxford Slavonic Papers* (for which there were valid practical reasons) was tempered by articles of Polish interest by Stanislas Kot in Volumes IV and VI and by Claude Backvis of Brussels University (also in Volume VI). Backvis was an erstwhile colleague of Boris Unbegaun at Brussels; Unbegaun had been elected Professor of Comparative Slavonic Philology at Oxford in 1953 and himself contributed several characteristically solid but elegant articles to the journal. The Polish component was later increased in an interesting way by another Warden of All Souls, John Sparrow, whose investigation of the work of the Polish Neo-Latin poet Casimir Sarbiewski (VIII) caused some controversy and elicited a rejoinder (XII).

As Editor, Sergey Aleksandrovich looked East as well as West. From Poland Professors Julian Krzyżanowski and Andrzej Walicki published articles in Volumes VIII and X respectively, and in 1957 Professor N. K. Gudzi of Moscow University became the journal's first Soviet contributor. He was followed by a remarkable list of compatriots—P. N. Berkov (VIII), V. I. Malyshev (XI), Yu. D. Levin (XII), M. P. Alekseev (XI), K. I. Chukovsky (XII), D. S. Likhachev (XIII), and V. M. Zhirmunsky (XIII)—the last four of whom came to the journal wearing, as it were, the robes of recently awarded Honorary Doctorates of Letters of the University.

From first to last the publication of documents was regarded as one of the chief services which contributors to *Oxford Slavonic Papers* could make to the advancement of learning. Apart from materials in Oxford, such as the Bodleian's glagolitic manuscripts (IV, V), many sources in private hands or in other British or overseas archives and libraries first saw the light in the journal. These included poems by Vyacheslav Ivanov (V, VII) and important collections of letters of Chekhov (IX), Herzen (III), Rainer Maria Rilke (IX), I. S. Turgenev (IX), and of Tsars Alexander II (XI), Alexander III (X, XI), and Nicholas II (X).

Finally, though articles have only once touched on Yugoslavia and Czechoslovakia (Czech archaeology was discussed in Volume XII by Sir Cecil Parrott, who contrived to combine scholarship with diplomacy while British Ambassador in Prague in the 1960s), the distinctly non-Slavonic Soviet Republic of Georgia received attention on two occasions. The first was in Volume VI in which Professor D. M. Lang of London University discussed Georgian studies at Oxford (including an account of the remarkable Wardrop Collection in the Bodleian); and the second, in Volume XII, in which another British Georgian expert, W. E. D. Allen, illuminated Tsar Boris Godunov's Georgian marriage projects. After these exotic flights it is only fair to add that *Oxford Slavonic Papers* under Sergey Aleksandrovich's editorship gave hospitality to more down-to-earth contributions. These included pioneer bibliographies of Valery Bryusov (XII) and of the novelist Leonid Leonov (XI), and—in the last volume to be published before the Founder-Editor's retirement—a list of theses in Slavonic studies accepted by British universities for higher degrees which showed not only that the first such degree was an Oxford one (in 1907), but also made plain the remarkable growth in graduate Slavonic studies in the University since Sergey Aleksandrovich's appointment to the Chair of Russian in 1945.

OXFORD SLAVONIC PAPERS, I-XIII

CONTENTS

VOLUME XII. 1965

VOLUME XIII. 1967

INDEX